STRATEGIES
FOR A
SUCCESSFUL
MARRIAGE
A STUDY GUIDE FOR MEN

E. GLENN WAGNER, PH. D.
WITH DIETRICH GRUEN

NAVPRESS

BRINGING TRUTH TO LIFE
NavPress Publishing Group
P.O. Box 35001, Colorado Springs, Colorado 80935

The Navigators is an international Christian organization. Our mission is to reach, disciple, and equip people to know Christ and to make Him known through successive generations. We envision multitudes of diverse people in the United States and every other nation who have a passionate love for Christ, live a lifestyle of sharing Christ's love, and multiply spiritual laborers among those without Christ.

NavPress is the publishing ministry of The Navigators. NavPress publications help believers learn biblical truth and apply what they learn to their lives and ministries. Our mission is to stimulate spiritual formation among our readers.

Printed in the United States of America

3 4 5 6 7 8 9 10 11 12 13 14 15 / 00 99 98 97 96

FOR A FREE CATALOG OF
NAVPRESS BOOKS & BIBLE STUDIES,
CALL 1-800-366-7788 (USA)
or 1-416-499-4615 (CANADA)

CONTENTS

INTRODUCTION

Almost no one is foolish enough to imagine he automatically deserves great success in any field of activity; yet almost everyone believes that he automatically deserves success in marriage.
   —SYDNEY J. HARRIS (1917–1986)

A marriage is like a long trip in a tiny rowboat: if one passenger starts to rock the boat, the other has to steady it; otherwise they will both go to the bottom together.
   —DAVID R. REUBEN (1933–)

Since the beginning of the century, divorce has increased some 700 percent. In 1960 there were four marriages to every one divorce. Now in North America there is one marriage for every divorce. Children born today have a 50 percent chance that before they reach the age of eighteen, they will see their parents separate. Our country fares worse than other industrialized nations: Great Britain (36 percent of all marriages end in divorce), France (a 22 percent divorce rate), Japan (17 percent rate), all the way down to Italy (which has a 4 percent divorce rate).

The Tragically High Divorce Rate Is Not the Real Problem
Countries with strict divorce laws like Italy might say with pride that their laws have stemmed the tide of the rising divorce rate. True enough, fewer Americans would legally divorce if tighter divorce laws were legislated and stricter religious prohibitions were enforced.
   But would legislative efforts alone bring about more truly

"successful" marriages? Or would there simply be more emotional divorces, marriage affairs, domestic cruelty, child abuse, murder and suicide cases? Such are the tragic, documented results of failed marriages that were not allowed legally (and mercifully) to terminate for the protection of those involved.

On the other hand, some have suggested that Americans could reduce the number of divorces by redefining the family and reducing the number of traditional marriages. The growth and acceptance of this regrettable social trend is also well-documented.

Both trends—stricter prohibitions of divorce and looser definitions of the family—miss the real problem. Although God hates divorce (Malachi 4:16), divorce per se is not the bogeyman. Divorce doesn't kill a marriage any more than a funeral director kills the corpse. Far more incriminating are the sinful ways that lead to a failed marriage that ends in divorce. That is, divorce doesn't kill and marriages don't fail; people do.

Conversely, marriages don't succeed or work; people succeed who work at marriage. That's because marriages do not necessarily make us any better or any worse, but marriage tests and reveals the character we bring to the marriage. As someone humorously put it, "Love is blind to faults, but marriage restores its sight." In which case, we concur with the witty retort, "Keep your eyes wide open before marriage, half shut afterwards." For that reason, some say, "It's better to choose your wife by ear than by eye."

This Book Is Not By, For, or About Perfect Partnership in Marriage

With fear and trepidation, we decided to write on the issue of marriage and men. We fear readers might perceive us as experts, having it all together. That simply is not the case. Just ask our wives.

Rather, this study guide reflects the mind-set of two men pursuing this adventure called marriage, along with you readers and other promise keepers. We simply share the struggles and lessons learned by trial and error and searching the Scriptures. What we've discovered, with the help of our wives and other men who hold us accountable, we share with you so that you might go and do likewise—share with your wives and meet with other men, holding one another accountable to strengthen your respective marriages.

Who Are You Authors, Anyway?

You'll get to know us soon enough as you study this book and read between the lines. Unless indicated otherwise from the context, the first person voice you hear in each narrative portion is Glenn's. Sometimes, for ease of reading and identification with the reader, the two of us blend the narrator's voice into a singular "I."

Generally, Glenn will lead out each chapter with personal stories and anecdotes to introduce hope and humor, so that men and women can enjoy their differences and build a successful marriage. He has a pastoral ministry, a growing speaking and conference ministry, and his own Promise Keepers ministry and network to draw from.

Dietrich draws from his experience in small groups and curriculum writing to pull together exercises meant for individual reflection, discussion with your spouse, and interaction with an accountability/support group of men. Anything we share about ourselves, about Glenn's wife, Susan, or Dietrich's wife, Suzanne, is with their blessing and permission, as we all desire to encourage others with what we have learned.

Should You Accept This Mission . . .

We grew up watching the television series *Mission: Impossible*. Perhaps you remember it. A group of highly skilled spies went where no other agency was able to penetrate. They redeemed hopeless situations through what was in their day "miraculous" technology. The opening scene was always the same: The leader of this spy agency, whose name was Jim, entered a phone booth, a restroom, or some other odd place and there played a recording, which described his clandestine mission. At the end of the tape, Jim was always given the option of accepting or rejecting the mission; then the tape would self-destruct.

This book is about a mission you can choose to accept or reject—a mission to take specific steps to strengthen your marriage. Although this book won't self-destruct over the next few minutes, by implementing the principles contained herein, you can avoid the sinful patterns and keep your relationships from self-destructing.

Take This Word from One Whose Marriage/Mission *Did* Self-Destruct

The former president of InterVarsity Christian Fellowship-USA, Dr. John W. Alexander, once approached Dietrich about writing a book on strengthening your marriage. Here's how he (Dietrich) recounts that "mission impossible."

I was offered this mission soon after I was separated and divorced in 1986. At that time any book coming out of my journal entries would have focused on surviving the end of a relationship. I could testify to the truths many have discovered about surviving and recovering from divorce. I was like the man who went over the edge of the Niagara Falls, was badly bruised and broken, but lived to tell about it.

However, the book that "Dr. A" wanted me to write, the one which was too difficult and painful for me to formulate at the time, was like a mission impossible. What he diagrammed on a napkin for me was a book focused on strengthening marriage. He pictured a boat with two at the oars. The book he diagrammed was not on divorce recovery (surviving Niagara Falls), nor was it about perfection ("row, row, your boat gently down the stream/ merrily, merrily, life is but a dream"). Rather, Dr. A's focus was on posting and heeding those warning signs (well upstream) to help other men avoid the strong undermining currents that swept one like me over the edge and into divorce as a last-resort remedy.

I agreed with Dr. A that his idea could make a worthwhile book, but not one I could write then or even now. At the time I was completely exhausted, psychologically and emotionally, from paddling upstream; so I took the easier way out, drifted with the current and took the plunge of divorce. Not until a latter-day mentor, Glenn Wagner, came along—with his own designs for a book on succeeding in marriage—could I fulfill the promise I made eight years earlier to John Alexander. What you hold in your hands is that book.

Are You Using What You Know?

The two of us agree that most divorces are foreseeable, predictable, and avoidable. Divorce is not inevitable—at least not at the top of the Niagara River, upstream in calmer waters, when it is still possible and prudent to resist the pull downstream, long before an exhausted couple comes to the brink. Signs posted on the Niagara River, well before the deadly falls, warn boaters: DO YOU HAVE AN ANCHOR? DO YOU KNOW HOW TO USE USE IT?

Most readers of our book will be in a similar boat—not always using what they know. You many not be heading over the falls of divorce, but neither are you enjoying a particularly fruitful marriage. Perhaps you are "dead in the water" or going nowhere in your marriage. Because of family pressures or doctrinal convictions, you would never divorce. But is your marriage truly succeeding? Cognitive knowledge alone is insufficient to survive a troubled marriage or to revive a listless one. We need solid models (strokes of encouragement and hope), usable skills (oars to paddle with), plus accountability and support (teamwork and lifejackets) to use what we learn together. That's what a group of men studying this book will get.

Anchors Away! Adventure Ahead!
To build a seaworthy marriage craft, men need more than relational skills. Christ must be Captain, Scripture the firm anchor, the Church a willing crew, and the marriage commitment a sound framework. That will hold us from the brink. We need practice paddling in calmer waters—to develop positive strokes, warm memories, and confidence in our boat.

Knowing how to rely on the Captain, the anchor, other crew members, and your partner will get you through troubled waters. The couple heading for dangerous waters or the false security of a pond needs the oars of faith for paddling upstream out of harm's way. Muscles of faith and hope, to believe God for rougher, deeper waters must be exercised well *before* facing the challenge of whitewater rapids.

In chapter 1 we post the warning signs which men in marriage boats ignore to their own peril. Seven warning signs are placed at the outset for you to heed and post for any friends who may be heading over the brink. Pay attention before it's too late. These dire warnings lie behind the positive strategies for a successful marriage outlined in chapters 2 through 8.

How This Guide Works
Each of the following chapters contains:

- several pages of text
- group discussion questions

■ actions you can take at home to put into practice what you're learning.

Ideally, participants should come to each group meeting having read the text. Alternatively, you can plan five or ten minutes at the beginning of your meeting for the men to read the text. You can cover the discussion adequately in forty-five minutes, although if you have more time, there's plenty to talk about!

Most of the chapters suggest things to discuss with your wife when you go home. Many include worksheets to help you evaluate your marriage and make practical what you have discussed. Sometimes you will make copies of a blank self-scoring worksheet for both yourself and your wife. You will fill them out separately and then discuss your results together. (Conditional permission is given to copy these worksheets for use in conjunction with your study of *Strategies for a Successful Marriage*. No pages in any other part of this book may be copied, nor may the worksheets be copied for any reason other than actual use with this book.)

When you return for your next group session, you'll have an opportunity to tell the group what happened when you talked with your wife. Some of you may never have raised such subjects with your wives before, but the group will be your cheerleading section and sounding board along the way.

Back from the brink, anchored in Scripture, with Christ at the helm, and heeding the warning signs of experience along the way, we can and will succeed at the adventure called marriage. Man the oars, work at your strokes, pace yourself in the weeks ahead. May you have a good time and enjoy the adventure of a lifetime.

1

ROUGH WATERS AND MARRIAGE BREAKERS AHEAD

THOUGHTS TO PONDER

[13]*He who conceals his sins does not prosper, but whoever confesses and renounces them finds mercy.* [14]*Blessed is the man who always fears the LORD, but he who hardens his heart falls into trouble.*
—SOLOMON (PROVERBS 28:13-14)

"Moses permitted you to divorce your wives because your hearts were hard. But it was not this way from the beginning."
—JESUS CHRIST (MATTHEW 19:8)

[12]*Therefore, as God's chosen people, holy and dearly loved, clothe yourselves with compassion, kindness, humility, gentleness and patience.* [13]*Bear with each other and forgive whatever grievances you may have against one another. Forgive as the Lord forgave you.* [14]*And over all these virtues put on love, which binds them all together in perfect unity.*
—THE APOSTLE PAUL (COLOSSIANS 3:12-14)

We know the widest thing in the universe is not space; it is the potential capacity of the human heart. Being made in the image of God, it is capable of almost unlimited extension in all directions. And one of the world's greatest tragedies is that we allow our hearts to shrink until there is room in them for little beside ourselves.
—A. W. TOZER (1897–1963)

Many signs along the river warn a couple in the marriage boat about the rocky shoals and the big falls. Before going over the edge and taking the plunge of actual or emotional divorce, we

are warned, "Turn Back—NOW!" Here are seven such signs to
post where you and your friends can see and heed them.

Warning Sign 1: Hard Heart
It may belabor the obvious to tell a child abuser that he has a
problem with anger. The most helpful time to point out and
address such a root problem is much sooner—upstream, *before*
hitting the rocks and the troubled waters.

So also with the hardhearted person for whom the unwanted
divorce is granted. It is most difficult for that person to hear that
his relationship deteriorated to the point of divorce because his
heart had become hard and unresponsive to the things of the
Lord. Yet that's what Solomon (Proverbs 28:13-14) and Jesus
(Matthew 19:8, Mark 10:5) are talking about.

One sure sign that we as husbands have hard hearts is that
we have lost compassion and forgiveness for our partner. Without
that tenderness, our words tear down rather than build up.

If I have hardened my heart, I will be more concerned about
getting my own needs met, forgetting about altruism and responsibility in the marriage. The vows once spoken are so soon forgotten. Deceived by a hardened heart (sin), we justify our
actions with excuses as old as creation. (Eve: "You ate the
apple." Adam: "But you gave it to me.") Sin is so deceitful, hard-
ening our hearts in the process, that we are unresponsive to any
needs and desires but our own.

Warning Sign 2: Excess Baggage
Sin, or hardness of heart, is the root problem in marriages that
are failing. Indeed, it is the root of all disease, injustice, and brokenness in the world (Mark 3:5). Yet sometimes there is no easy,
one-to-one correlation between a particular marital failure and
one particular sin. That's because sin is not only private, moral
rebellion with its own set of individual consequences; sin is also
manifest in systemic evil and abuse from generation to generation. When we suffer severe sin at the hands of others, we can't
help but bring brokenness into our marriage, rocking and sometimes capsizing the marriage boat, often leading its victims into
marital stress or even divorce.

In such extreme cases, professional or pastoral counseling
can sometimes help the affected family members shed layers of

guilt and other ballast from the past, thus helping to float their overburdened boat. At other times the brokenness is so severe and the coping skills so limited that the marriage boat is half-submerged when you enter into it. Such a broken, leaky vessel is not seaworthy to begin with and should stay close to shore.

Warning Sign 3: Unresolved Conflicts
Unresolved arguments build up over time and spill over in unsightly, injurious ways. Before you know it, your leaky marriage boat has taken in too much water and sinks. When intense disagreements become heated arguments, generating more heat than light, real communication ceases. People who wear on, tear down, even strike another soon cause their partner to abandon ship for safety's sake, rather than risk staying on board.

Some couples love to argue, they say, "because kissing and making up is so much fun to do." But long-term effects of that pattern, if uncorrected, are not fun. Others say, "If you *never* argue, you're not really communicating." I have difficulty finding a biblical rationale for that. Still others contend, "You need a good argument so that you can release all the tension that's been built up in your marriage." Again I ask, where in Scripture does God invite us to release tension by inflicting that tension and pain upon someone else?

On the contrary, here's what I see in Scripture: "A brother helped is like a strong city, but quarreling is like the bars of a castle" (see Proverbs 18:19). Evidently, a pattern of arguing is so destructive that it actually builds castle-like barriers between the two of you, even if apparently harmless at the time. Unresolved conflicts, especially ones we husbands perpetuate or get angry over, breed walls of resentment in our wives.

Continuous arguing normally results from unprocessed emotions that "build up and blow up," resulting in injurious words or outbursts of anger. "A hot-tempered man stirs up dissension, but a patient man calms a quarrel" (Proverbs 15:18). If not under your conscious control, anger can ignite a rather cool disagreement into something heated and destructive.

Man's anger does not reflect the righteousness of God (James 1:20), nor the compassion of Jesus Christ. "A fool's lips bring him strife, and his mouth invites a beating. A fool's mouth is his undoing, and his lips are a snare to his soul" (Proverbs 18:6-7).

Only "fools" enter into contentious arguments rather than real communication and thus jeopardize their relationship.

Warning Sign 4: Unmet Expectations

Men are easily bent out of shape over what we deem our "needs." We seem to enjoy the chase more than the catch. Many restless men never come to the place of being content with the wife of their youth. The Bible warns about the danger of not meeting the needs of your spouse (1 Corinthians 7:3-5,9) and of not being content with her (Proverbs 5:15-20).

There are two sides to this signpost. On the front side, I should not place unrealistic, dream-like expectations upon my spouse. No one person should be expected to meet all the needs we have. Hidden, undeclared expectations (patterned after, or in reaction to, our parents' marriage or a former marriage) can booby-trap even the best of intentions in marriage.

The flip side is this: I should find out what my wife's expectations are and then commit myself to doing everything within my power to meet them—not just the physical and financial needs, but also the spiritual and emotional expectations. Meeting the mutual and realistic expectations we have for marriage is part of the "oneness" that defines a biblical union (Genesis 2:24, Matthew 19:5, 1 Corinthians 6:16-17, Ephesians 5:31).

Only superhuman spouses can go for long periods of time without their physical, emotional, and spiritual needs being met. Whatever expectations you and your spouse have, they should be distinguished and prioritized if you hope to fulfill them and thus avoid chilly waters.

Warning Sign 5: Unreasonable Demands

Many men are perfectionists who place such high expectations upon their wives that they can never measure up. This ideal-mate syndrome is pictured in the commercials we watch. For once, wouldn't it be nice to see a slightly overweight woman trying to sell you a car or after-shave lotion? Wouldn't it be great to have the workout videos feature real rundown people (like many of us) with a mid-life paunch? Ever see any people with blemishes beaming at you on the newsstand and magazine rack?

Such made-for-the-male-fantasy images soon send us home to our less-than-perfect mate, saying, "My wife doesn't measure up." (Get real, guys, neither do you!) Is your wife a victim of unreasonable demands?

The Bible warns husbands about trapping our wives with such unreasonable demands. Instead, a husband is to live with his wife in an understanding or considerate way, giving honor and respect to her (1 Peter 3:7). Husbands, "rejoice in the wife of your youth" (Proverbs 5:18). Instead, we long to trade her in for a younger model with new or better features. (Remember, you're not getting any younger, either.)

You may not be trading partners, but many men engage in something similar which could lead to the same result: we want to remake her, to perfect her, to conform her to some stereotyped or TV-hyped image of beauty. Perhaps unwittingly, you've made your life partner ("for better or worse") into your change project ("get better or else"). Such unreasonable demands only tear down your marriage and lead you further downstream to the brink of divorce.

If you find yourself this far downstream—to warning sign 5—immediately drop anchor or paddle upstream. In other words, stop trying to change your wife. If you keep trying to change her, you'll drive the two of you crazy. Use the great change agent we have in prayer, which changes us more than anything else. God is the great mover of people's hearts. Let Him work in a marvelous way. (For more on prayer to God as a way to lower your demands on the wife and build your mate's self-image instead, see chapter 8.)

Warning Sign 6: "Irreconcilable Differences"
Rather than put forth the effort God requires of husbands to love their wives, we often decide that differences between us are what the courts call "irreconcilable" or insurmountable. At this point in the river of life you have passed all the other warning signs: Hard Heart, Excess Baggage, Unresolved Conflicts, Unmet Expectations, and Unreasonable Demands. Now you are down river at the point of no return—so you think. The truth about marriage is far worse and more hopeful: our whole lives are irreconcilable.

Opposites *attract*—that combustible chemistry is often what begins a marriage. Opposites also *attack*—but that need not end a marriage. Opposites can work together to strengthen their marriage and attack, instead, the very forces that drive them apart. In this regard, wrote Sydney Smith two centuries ago, "Marriage is like a pair of shears, so joined that they cannot be separated; often moving in opposite directions, yet always punishing any one who comes between them."

Two people with different natures and needs, living together in harmony under the same roof for many years—that is the adventure of marriage. That is a divine gift, not a human achievement. Only by the common grace of God and the uncommon love of the Lord Jesus will that happen. Only a marriage *triangle*—one composed of a man, a woman, and God—investing all they are and have—will reach its full potential.

Warning Sign 7: Unforgiving Spirit
The last warning sign before going over the brink is this one. More than anything else, the anchor that will keep you from going over the precipice of divorce is forgiveness. We need to grant it, and we need to receive it. As Dr. James Dobson says, "A good marriage is not one where perfection reigns; it is a relationship where a healthy perspective overlooks a multitude of 'unresolvables.'"

We know that we're supposed to be kind, tender-hearted, gentle, patient, forgiving (Colossians 3:12-14). Such virtues are not feelings we conjure up or actions we do only when we feel like it. Husbands, "clothe yourselves" with these virtues, and as a coverall "put on love." Whether you want to or not, you get dressed every morning. For the same reason—whether we feel like it or not—we should wear this spiritual attire/attitude toward our wives. Such love not only covers (holds together) your virtues but also covers (forgives) a multitude of sins and "irreconcilable" differences (Proverbs 10:12, Romans 13:8-10, 1 Peter 4:8).

We wouldn't think of going to work undressed or without the proper clothing. Why then do we wear such offensive or "devil-may-care-but-I-don't" attire at home? Why can't we bring ourselves to say, "Honey, will you forgive me? I'm sorry."

I know it's all too easy to say those words and not mean them. Repentance, or change of direction, is involved with forgiveness. "He who covers over an offense promotes love, but whoever repeats the matter separates close friends" (Proverbs

17:9). Human pride keeps us from seeking another's forgiveness sincerely; that same pride also keeps us from forgiving our spouse. Yet God says "it is to our glory to overlook an offense" (Proverbs 19:11).

Remember the example of Christ, because that can melt even the hardest of hearts (Ephesians 4:32, Colossians 3:13). He takes our hardened hearts, all our excess baggage, all our unresolved conflicts, all our unmet expectations, all our unreasonable demands, even our irreconcilable differences, and forgives it all. But with an unforgiving spirit, we can not appreciate all that Christ did for us, because "if you do not forgive men their sins, your Father will not forgive your sins" (Matthew 6:15).

WHAT DO YOU THINK?

1. What were you pondering as the seven warning signs whizzed by?

   □ Whew! Thank God I didn't marry someone like that.
   □ Help! I did marry someone like that and I'm drowning!!
   □ I may have missed a sign or two, but I've stabilized the marriage boat, avoided the brink, and am treading water safely.
   □ I have trouble reading the signs; this chapter raised key questions.
   □ Wagner and Gruen missed the boat on this one.
   □ I was thinking of certain warnings my parents gave me.
   □ I ponder what to teach my children about choosing a mate and succeeding at marriage.

2. Imagine yourself as the proud father of a bride- or groom-to-be, or as the author of a book about succeeding in marriage. Based on what you have learned so far from your own marriage or that of your parents, what is your prescription for making your children's marriages as "seaworthy" or "divorce-resistant" as possible? (See also question 9.)

3. As part of each chapter we pose study questions based on Scripture. Usually we reflect on and develop further the keynote Scripture displayed at the outset of your reading notes. This time around, we give you the biblical prescription for successful marriage found in Colossians 3:12-14 (at the beginning of this chapter). Use this passage as a checklist of virtues for you to try on for size, or to grow into.

   a. Which of those clothing items (Christian virtues) suit you well? Which one suits you to a "T"?

   b. Which clothing items represent virtues tucked away in a closet somewhere, paraded out and worn only on special occasions, such as anniversaries or Valentine's Day?

4. Where do you personally go to find models of a successful marriage?

   ☐ Right or wrong, I've learned most of what I know from my parents.
   ☐ An older couple has helped me a lot.
   ☐ I combine the best of what I see presented on TV, in the movies, and in literature.
   ☐ The other members of this group have been a big help to me.
   ☐ Other (name it):

5. How is your particular marriage like a "pair of shears"? (That is, how are you and your spouse different, moving in opposite directions? At what points are you both inseparably attached? What has come between the two of you that gets you and your spouse to attack it together—like a pair of shears moving forward in the same direction?)

6. Ask yourself: Have I been exhibiting attitudes and actions that have been tearing down my wife rather than building

her up? Which of the seven warning signs do I want to take to heart for myself and learn more about during the course of this study? (Your answer to this two-part question will be used in the positive, upbuilding exercise below.)

7. This exercise is for you to rehearse with the men in your group, who will then cheer you on as you do it for real later on with your spouse.

   Consider the one area in which you've been tearing down your wife or rocking the boat (question 6). "Name it and tame it," and "Say it or play it," as marriage counselors advise. That is, self-awareness and confession of the particular marriage breaker tends to calm troubled waters and stabilize your boat. In groups of two, three, or four men, take turns naming it or confessing it. This is a role play. Without giving too much of the context or self-justification, simply tell one or more of the men in your group what you want to work on during this stage of your marriage.

We just introduced once-over-lightly some pretty heavy-duty warnings. If you failed to heed these warnings earlier in life and inadvertently chose to marry someone who is rocking your boat, all is not lost; divorce is never inevitable. The help and hope we offer in the rest of this book will make change possible. The cycles and patterns of past generations can be broken.

Make a commitment among yourselves to support the other men on this adventure of faith and marriage building. As you read chapter 2 in preparation for the next session, begin thinking how you set goals at work and how you might also do that in your marriage. Developing a game plan or "Family Mission Statement" is introduced next week and will be explored further, along with other success strategies for marriage, in the course of the next seven sessions. Enjoy!

TRY IT AT HOME
This section in each chapter includes ways for you to put into practice what you have been discussing with your group.

8. With the role play (question 7) and biblical dress rehearsal (question 3) to give you confidence and something to wear, now go home and set a date with your wife to make amends. You've been convicted of it by the Spirit of God and you want her forgiveness. However, you also want her encouragement and prayer, as you seek to bring change to your life together.

    Do something nice to set the stage: Get a babysitter for the kids. Take her out to dinner—someplace private. Once there, acknowledge to her what you have been doing that has jeopardized the health of your marriage. Suggest an area you want to work on and invite her to help make a good marriage better.

9. Take this book home and teach your children well.

    We recognize that you want a successful marriage for yourself, or you wouldn't have picked this book to read and study with a group of men. However, there is another intended audience for this book. All of us with children will want successful marriages for them. You can help yourself or your children enter into a divorce-resistant marriage if you and they heed certain early warning signals. Anyone who knowingly chooses a dubious or even dangerous person for their spouse chooses a marriage prone to pain and probable divorce. If the choice is still yours or your child's to make, we advise not getting in the same boat with that person.

    Teach your children well. Clear "danger ahead" warning signals should caution you about getting in the marriage boat with these boat-rockers:

    ■ Anyone who resorts to physical violence, chronic fighting, or must-win arguments during courtship (it will only get worse).
    ■ Anyone from an alcoholic or abusive household who refuses to get help for their problem (alcoholic or addictive personalities can be charming, appealing to your need to be needed, but the sins of the fathers do pass from generation to generation).
    ■ Anyone you feel sorry for or want to change (marriage

may be an institution, but it is not a reform school).

■ Anyone you are marrying out of guilt (because of premarital sex or an out-of-wedlock child), because guilt is a terrible glue for a lasting marriage.

■ Anyone who is unfaithful, sexually, during the courtship (it's better to break off the engagement on such grounds than a marriage).

■ Anyone who is not ready psychologically or emotionally to separate from their parents (if you don't "leave" before you "cleave and become one flesh," it's as if those parents are in bed with you).

■ Anyone who recently comes off a separation or divorce, or even one who has just broken off a long engagement (such "rebound relationships" are transitional and short-lived; better to wait for God's healing to take full effect).

■ Anyone your friends or relatives consistently warn you about (because "love" may blind us to serious character flaws of another).

a. What boat-rockers would you add to this list?

b. From your own experience, are there any points you can identify with?

c. These points obviously need to be expanded upon and qualified when talking to a friend or relative already in a boat-rocking relationship. Map out and pray about what you will say. Rehearse this speech with another man or your wife.

2

MEN DON'T ASK DIRECTIONS
(But we will develop a game plan and follow it)

HOW DID IT GO?

1. In groups of three or four men, debrief on the progress you made on last session's homework assignment. Limit this discussion to fifteen minutes so you'll have time to cover the rest of this session. If you find you need more time for debriefing, plan to meet together again after this session.

    a. Were you able to make time with your wife to make amends?

    b. Were you convicted of a trouble spot by the Spirit of God for which you asked and received forgiveness?

    c. Was she able to offer encouragement and prayer as you seek to change your lives together?

    d. Is this something you never want to try again, or something you want to make into a habit? Explain.

THOUGHTS TO PONDER

As for me and my house, we will serve the LORD.
    —JOSHUA (JOSHUA 24:15, RSV)

Commit to the LORD whatever you do, and your plans will succeed. . . . In his heart a man plans his course, but the LORD

*determines his steps. . . . Many are the plans in a man's heart, but it is
the LORD's purpose that prevails.*
    —SOLOMON (PROVERBS 16:3,9; 19:21)

*A mission statement has to be operational, otherwise it's just
good intentions. . . . One of our most common mistakes is to make
the mission statement into a kind of hero sandwich of good intentions.
It has to be simple and clear. . . . A mission is not . . . impersonal.
I have never seen anything being done well unless people were
committed.*
    —PETER F. DRUCKER

To establish a plan or set goals for a marriage partnership strikes
fear into many hearts. I share the fear you may be experiencing.
Governing my family by principle and purpose—not by crisis
thinking, a quick-fix solution, or mood swings—is not an area in
which I excel.

My ministry and professional life I run by a DayTimer; my
to-do list is prioritized down to the very minute. Under crunch
times, I have been known to apportion projects I am working on
a certain number of minutes, then shift from project to project
under the watchful and motivating eye of an alarm clock or oven
timer. Productivity is the key, as I aim to finish each day with a
smaller stack of papers and correspondence than when I began.

With this kind of time management, you'd think I would run
my home life this way. *Au contraire!* As soon as I leave my office,
a strange transformation takes place. I find myself suddenly
unmotivated to map out a plan. I often come to the eve of a
vacation without deciding where we are going or what we will
do. At times I feel that life, especially recreation, simply has to
"just happen."

I often take this what-will-be-will-be tendency into my marriage and family life, as well. Many couples begin as we did: we
spent time talking about the future. When my wife, Susan, and I
decided to marry, we discussed certain goals: what God wanted
for us; my need to finish college, seminary and grad school; and
my call to pastoral ministry. I believed then, as I do now, that
engaged couples must ask the hard questions *before* entering
marriage. Otherwise, you wrestle with unanswered questions or
avoidable mistakes the rest of your life.

All of the couples with whom I have done premarital counseling were filled with enthusiasm and excitement, exuding love and hope for the future. However, I have also watched many couples over time lose touch with their priorities and good intentions. Pursuing careers, raising children, getting involved at church, establishing a foothold in this uncertain economy—that all begins to take its toll on the best laid plans of nice young men. Falling out of love was not "planned," nor was it done with malice or intent. It simply happened. Yet as many have pointed out, "failing to plan" means "planning to fail."

How a Mission Statement Works

Process is more important than product in this regard. The very process of planning and goal-setting helps keep one's marriage and family life in check by establishing a precedent for nurturing one's relationship. The precedent-setting plan I'm talking about is not some "Lifetime Strategic Plan," covering forty years of your life together, over a hundred pages in length, with an executive summary to be presented to one's guardian angel or in-laws.

Rather, what I envision for men who are promise keepers is this: an ongoing assessment of growth areas in your marriage, an exploration of future choices, and a determination to go the distance. Although intricate plans are not called for, your plan should establish a sense of direction and give enough specifics to measure hoped-for progress.

The ultimate goal Susan and I have for our marriage is to be more in love with each other at the end of our days than on the day we got married. Our mission statement reads: "To be committed to grow together in God's grace and live out that grace in all our relationships."

■ *Committed* involves a resolution to stick with it and a realization that we are in process.

■ *Grow together* means we recognize that we are in partnership: as Susan grows in her relationship with God, that enhances and encourages my walk with the Lord, and vice versa.

■ *In God's grace* implies we want to know and appreciate more of God in our lives; by His grace, or unmerited favor, our relationship is strengthened.

■ *Live out that grace in all our relationships* means being salt and light in fulfilling our role in the family, through our ministries, and in our community.

Dietrich's personal mission statement reads: "To communicate good news at the point of human need through whatever means, media, or models are entrusted to my care—in family, church or marketplace." He spells that out in terms of his various roles, for example:

■ To be a growing disciple of Jesus Christ.
■ To be a loving husband of Sue.
■ To be a nurturing father of Mark, Eric, and Matt.
■ To maintain hobbies, physical fitness, and non-work interests as a check on my tendency to overwork.
■ To be an effective writer/editor of specialty Bibles and Christian education materials.

You could also state your mission in terms of simple action verbs: "To love each other . . . To steward our stuff . . . To worship together in Christ . . . To support one another in mission." Or you can state your mission, as thousands have, in terms of the Seven Promises of a Promise Keeper (see back matter, page 115). With some such ultimate goal always in mind, the wise married couple will seek to draft and implement a plan to get there from here.

Do take advantage of what is available through your church or other ministry opportunities, such as a marriage conference or a couples' retreat. Map out times of refreshment and renewal. Go with a small group from your church, perhaps even the group of you studying this book, or simply get away as a couple on your own. However or whenever you do it, you will greatly benefit from taking extended time to renew yourselves and deal with issues that you have left unresolved for lack of planning.

There is no one "right" way for everyone to make plans. Whatever works best for you is what you should follow. Some people like intricate detail, others prefer concise strategic statements, still others want only bare bones or general parameters. Have fun as you and your partner experiment with putting into words the mission that you detect God has appointed for your life together.

Buyer Beware

In writing a mission statement, be careful. Nothing is more hazardous to your marriage than a high-sounding mission, filled with idealistic sentiments that can raise hopes and expectations, only to have them crushed somewhere down the line. As you prepare to work on your mission statement, bear in mind that goals for success in marriage are easier promised than kept. The temptation to promise your spouse the moon often increases when you're gathering with your friends, or even in an intimate setting with her.

The fact that you and your spouse have different personalities, gifts, and desires means that you must work on your mission together. If you simply formulate it yourself, your plan will be limited, even biased, by your own perspective, and she will not buy into it. As you work at building consensus for a win-win agreement, you will discover the document will be more enduring if its language is inclusive and its goals general. You'll want to convey a broad vision of the values you hold dear, leaving specifics to be spelled out from year to year.

The only way your wife will buy into the mission statement is if she participates in formulating it. Make sure her ideas are fully included; otherwise, when things go awry, she will be quick to point out your lack of foresight and planning. A shared mission statement has an inspiring, energizing effect and wide-ranging impact. A sense of pride and teamwork will, in itself, enhance your relationship and hold you both accountable for its fulfillment.

Family mission statements allow for power-sharing that prohibits anyone from making unilateral or random decisions contrary to your stated mission and goals. In doing this exercise, you make a mutual commitment to journey in the same direction. Family mission statements also bring focus, keeping extraneous "nice things to do" from dissipating your strengths in various unrelated directions. Motivation without focus stirs up dust and produces movement—but few useful results.

A shared vision requires concentrated "active listening" (see role-play exercise, chapter 4, page 62, for more on this). This is no time for speech-making or dictation. Although you may have the ability to persuade, that will not generate a shared vision that your wife will be comfortable pursuing with you. I cannot stress enough the need to listen, listen, and listen. When you think you're done, listen even more.

Listening will begin to inspire confidence and respect in your wife, which in turn will inspire you in seeking to serve and to lead. With this "buyer beware" caveat in mind, here then are a few more suggestions for tackling this project:

Set Aside Time for Serious, Sincere Evaluation

Step back to see where you are and where you're heading. The "Inventory of Strengths and Weaknesses" on pages 33-38 is designed to help you evaluate. Try to get away for a day or two with your spouse to work through it. This is not a one-shot deal or an overnighter. Thoughtful analysis, personal introspection, joint discussion, mutual submission, and a few rewrites will likely be involved. If kids are a problem in your getting away, try parking them with their grandparents or another couple with similar-age kids on a swap basis. If you cannot swing that, simply sequester yourself within your own house, turn off the TV, turn on the answering machine, and do everything else you can to protect uninterrupted time for this.

Come Together with Your Spouse for a Time of Discussion

After each partner completes his or her own copy of the inventory worksheet separately, come together to discuss the various growth areas within your marriage. Set the ground rules: no criticism; no defensiveness; no *why* questions meant only to badger the other person out of his or her feelings. (Feelings don't have justification; they just are.) Each is entitled to his or her own perception about whether or not the relationship is strong or weak in a particular area. Don't be surprised if you and your mate differ in your responses to the same statements. Also, don't let false guilt weigh you down, but use this inventory to bring conviction in your plan and goal-setting for a successful marriage.

Develop a Plan to Grow Your Marriage

Once you have evaluated your marriage and talked through your different perspectives on the inventory questions, compile those issues that you agree need to be addressed and worked on. The areas needing the most attention will probably fall into at least five areas: *spiritual, personal, family/parental, relational,* and *financial.*

Try to make your goals specific, attainable, and measurable, so that throughout the coming months you can chart the progress you make. To help find out if a goal is attainable or not, you need to attach to each goal several "action steps." These are specific activities or tasks that, if completed, will contribute to the fulfillment of that goal. Action steps are written to answer questions like "How much?" and "When?"

For *spiritual* growth, some of the tasks would be: prayer times together, study of God's Word, family worship, finding a regular church home, getting involved in a Bible study.

Personal goals would cover educational pursuits, hobbies, vocational concerns, physical exercise and well-being.

Under *family/parental* goals, be sure to respect the individuality of each child and set specific goals for each one, rather than lumping all your children together. Also state any goals you have for extended family members and their needs.

Relational goals deal with interpersonal skills, Christian virtues (remember those "clothing items" from the last session?), the sexual relationship, spending time together, and outside social relationships and activities.

Financial goals include lifestyle or comfort level choices; funding for college and/or retirement living options; pensions, IRA's or other savings plans; current debt-reduction.

While these five are the categories we give you to think through on the worksheet, "Developing a Family Mission Statement," you may want to organize your mission statement according to the various roles you take on: disciple of Christ, husband, father, son/brother, neighbor, student, kingdom worker/change agent.

Put Your Action Steps on the Calendar
Once you have brainstormed on all the above goals, build a weekly task or to-do list. To make sure you will actually get around to it, make a calendar in which you schedule these action steps. Be sure to distinguish between "urgent" and "important." (For more about making time for each other, see chapter 7, page 93.)

Take Your Mission Statement Out for a Test Drive
When you get behind the wheel of your mission statement and

put the rubber to the road, several test questions will help you refine the rough draft into something more enduring and inspiring:

- Does it actually inspire your performance and define your character?
- Does it bring out the best in you and yours?
- Does it squeeze you into the world's mold and someone else's agenda, or does it fit you and stretch you?
- Does it transform your thinking and rev up your vision?
- Does it rekindle love and good works that fulfill your covenant promises?

WHAT DO YOU THINK?

2. What's your reaction to being told to apply to your marriage the same kind of strategic planning that men use all the time at work?

☐ I can set goals at work, so I also can set goals for my marriage.

☐ I hate planning; it takes away all spontaneity in relationships.

☐ Now I see why I have been falling short in my marriage.

☐ I have trouble making plans and setting goals in all areas of my life, so I need help being intentional about succeeding in my marriage.

☐ Wagner and Gruen left me on their drawing boards; their ideas don't fit me or my marriage partner.

☐ This confirms one of the strategies that already works for me in my marriage.

3. Imagine yourself in a virtual reality machine which offers you an opportunity to redo the lifestyle choices, the ethical dilemmas, and the road less traveled in your marriage. In this fantastic scenario, you make the choices that are right for you; you end up scripting your marriage from the very beginning the way you want it to turn out. The only given in this scenario is that the woman you marry in virtual reality is the same one you have now in actual reality. Other than that, you can virtually replay and plan out the rest of your marriage from day one.

a. What choices and plans did you make in marriage that you would not redo for anything?

b. Which choices in your marriage would you like to redo, or what plans did you shelve that you would like to reconsider if only you could?

4. Proverbs provides a biblical perspective on the need for planning in marriage, as for all of life. Yet proverbial wisdom also warns that reliance on planning and goal-setting alone will not accomplish God's purpose for your marriage. To find out why and how that is the case, read the following from Proverbs:

> The plans of the righteous are just, but the advice of the wicked is deceitful. (12:5)
> Plans fail for lack of counsel, but with many advisers they succeed. (15:22)
> To man belong the plans of the heart, but from the LORD comes the reply of the tongue. (16:1)
> Commit to the LORD whatever you do, and your plans will succeed. (16:3)
> In his heart a man plans his course, but the LORD determines his steps. (16:9)
> Many are the plans in a man's heart, but it is the LORD'S purpose that prevails. (19:21)
> Make plans by seeking advice; if you wage war, obtain guidance. (20:18)
> The plans of the diligent lead to profit as surely as haste leads to poverty. (21:5)

a. Which of the above uses of planning are true in your marriage?

b. Which of the above aspects of planning have you neglected to the detriment of your marriage?

5. Look over the "Inventory of Strengths and Weaknesses" (pages 33-38). Go over the instructions together to be sure they make sense to everyone in the group.

   You have permission to photocopy this inventory for your own and your wife's use (see page 10). If time permits and each group member has already made a blank copy for his wife, you can start filling out your own copies within this session.

6. Look over the worksheet "Developing a Family Mission Statement" (pages 39-40). Your leader should make sure everyone in the group understands the instructions.

TRY IT AT HOME

Make a date—or several dates—for when you will sit down with your wife and do the following.

7. a. Give your wife a copy of the "Inventory of Strengths and Weaknesses" and keep one for yourself. Each of you should fill it out separately.

   b. Meet with your wife to compare your answers to the inventory. Remember the instructions: no criticism; no defensiveness; etc.

   c. Ask yourself and your wife which of the areas of weakness in your marriage that you have identified should be the one you will focus on during the rest of this group study. It is not more spiritual to choose fifteen areas. For starters, select one or two and be faithful in a little before you take on more.

   d. Make copies of the worksheet, "Developing a Family Mission Statement" for yourself and your wife. (You may want to enlarge the copies for more writing space.) Each of you should fill it out separately. Afterward, merge your statements into one master plan.

INVENTORY OF STRENGTHS AND WEAKNESSES
In Spiritual, Personal, Family/Parental, Relational, and Financial Areas

This inventory, covering five areas of your marital relationship, may help you and your partner gain a better idea of strengths to build on and weaknesses to work on. Answer each of these true or false. A self-scoring key follows the inventory.

A. Relational
1. I have some jealousies or bitterness about previous partners I or my partner may have had, which I carry as "baggage" into our marriage. T F

2. I have no conflicts about keeping the priority of our marriage ahead of work or the children. T F

3. I proudly introduce my partner to others on every occasion imaginable—at work, at the club, with new friends, etc. T F

4. I am satisfied with our sexual relationship. T F

5. I often withdraw in silence or blow up in anger, forcing my partner to figure out why and to do something to please or appease me. T F

6. I frequently ignore or discount my partner's opinion or feelings in favor of mine. T F

B. Family/Parental
1. My partner and I agree on the ways we discipline all the children, even those with special needs; they have not come between us. T F

2. All the parents and grandparents involved are equally accepting of our children and any children we have from previous marriages. T F

3. My partner and I do not have a common agenda for "family night." We frequently disagree on extracurricular fun or time-sharing as a family. T F

4. After allowing for age and gender differences, my partner and I treat all of our children alike. T F

5. I have no concerns with how any of our children are turning out—emotionally, physically, socially, or spiritually. T F

6. All of our children get along well with each other and with schoolmates, even with their stepbrothers or stepsisters. T F

C. Financial
1. My partner and I did not fully disclose our respective financial situations to each other before we got married. T F

2. My partner and I agree on how the money should be spent each month, with mutual accountability and submission on all major purchases. T F

3. I control most of the finances and make my partner account for all expenditures. T F

4. My partner and I have not fully discussed or resolved our differences on income goals, insurance plans, investment strategies, retirement accounts, charitable giving, and lifestyle comforts that suit us. T F

5. My partner and I each have our own spending money, regardless of who earns it, with no accountability to the other for discretionary items. T F

6. My partner and I do not have a plan for what to do if disability, pregnancy, economic downturn, or personal lifestyle choices were to force us to live on much less money. T F

D. Personal

1. I have different ideas than my partner of what to do for "fun" or leisure, which has led to independent pursuits of hobbies, social friends, exercise, and recreation. T F

2. Despite the amount of time together, I enjoy only a minimum of playfulness with my partner; even activities on our joint calendar tend to leave us feeling very separate. T F

3. My partner and I have developed some common pursuits of pleasure that have us feeling secure, laughing again, and interacting more. T F

4. My partner and I are free to develop separate friends, hobbies, and recreational pursuits without having always to account for our time. T F

5. My partner and I have difficulty agreeing on where to go, what to do, even whether to go on vacations. T F

6. I do not have separate interests from my partner; we enjoy doing virtually everything together. T F

E. Spiritual

1. Even on days I do not feel love for members of my family, I am able to affirm differences, bear with one another, and forgive the hurt. T F

2. I have problems admitting when I am wrong, asking and receiving forgiveness from my partner. T F

3. I have great freedom with my partner in taking everything to the Lord in prayer. T F

4. When I struggle with issues of faith, my partner is not necessarily privy to that. T F

5. My partner and I have not blended our different worship styles or spiritual needs and gifts; one or the other of us gives more to or gets more from weekly worship services, leaving me feeling dissatisfied. T F

6. My partner and I have our own devotional lives and regularly share our growing edge and/or biblical insights with one another. T F

Scoring Key for the Strengths and Weaknesses Inventory

A.1. Give yourself 0 points if True, 1 point if False. If you or your partner has a negative relationship with a former spouse or romantic interest, this may indicate unresolved issues that could undermine your current marriage if left unaddressed. Likewise, jealousy or anger about one of your spouse's former relationships could spark trouble.

A.2. Give yourself 1 point if True, 0 points if False. If one of you is having an "affair with work," the other can feel resentful that her expectations or his promises were not met; the same can be said of child-centered marriages.

A.3. Give yourself 1 point if True, 0 points if False. If your partner is not someone you respect and admire enough to introduce publicly, then you must ask yourself if you are anything more than lovers, domestic help, or financial security.

A.4. Give yourself 1 point if True, 0 points if False. Dissatisfaction in the sexual relationship can be symptomatic of many other trouble spots: lack of trust, poor communication, unrealistic expectations, guilt, anger. Better to ask than to guess.

A.5. Give yourself 0 points if True, 1 point if False. Emotional withdrawal or clamming up and later blowing up can be ways of controlling or manipulating, even abusing, the other person. We control through moodiness, anger, and threats.

A.6. Give yourself 0 points if True, 1 point if False. We also control through denial of the other's perceptions. In its extreme form, this measure of control can be crazy-making.

B.1. Give yourself 1 point if True, 0 points if False. A united front is important in matters of discipline. Although you will disagree privately, when presenting the family line, you must be prepared to back up one another's disciplinary strategies.

B.2. Give yourself 1 point if True, 0 points if False. Extended families can be a source of either stress or support—depending on how accepting the parents and grandparents are of the various branches of the family.

B.3. Give yourself 0 points if True, 1 point if False. Having no agreed-upon "family time" may signal lack of coordinated planning, lack of negotiating skill, lack of creativity, or some other lack. Family time requires certain sacrifices and structure.

B.4. Give yourself 1 point if True, 0 points if False. Equal justice for all, applicability of rules and consequences for all, no special gifts or privileges for one—such are the grounds for harmonious family relationships. However, no child wants to be lumped with the others and treated the same, as each one deserves special attention. You may want to reverse the scoring and give yourself a point for loving kids *uniquely*, if not *equally*.

B.5. Give yourself 0 points if True, 1 point if False. Having NO concerns for a child's well-being may not be a good thing, if lack of concern stems from ignorance or apathy on the part of parents or no honest communication from the child. However, if you have reason to be TRULY concerned, reverse the scoring and give yourself a point for a major problem area.

B.6. Give yourself 1 point if True, 0 points if False. After allowing for normal healthy sibling rivalry, be on guard, lest tension and conflict between the children, especially in a blended family, stir up friction between you and your partner.

C.1. Give yourself 0 points if True, 1 point if False. Full disclosure before the marriage starts paves the way for better future planning and trust once the marriage is consummated, children enter the picture, and certain hardships hit (see C.6.).

C.2. Give yourself 1 point if True, 0 points if False. Both free-spenders and frugal savers need to be mutually accountable in some agreed-upon system of checks and balances. Money fights may signal something else is wrong in the marriage.

C.3. Give yourself 0 points if True, 1 point if False. One-sided decision making on money matters is a form of control and abuse.

C.4. Give yourself 0 points if True, 1 point if False. Since women outlive men in most marriages, and since many women are kept in the dark about money matters, wives should take on more money-management responsibility and authority.

C.5. Give yourself 1 point if True, 0 points if False. Having your own money to spend, no matter how small the allowance or principal, is psychologically, if not financially, important for everyone in the family.

C.6. Give yourself 0 points if True, 1 point if False. Having a contingency plan for doing with less income is a healthy, prudent exercise to do—a prerequisite for knowing what to do should a sudden financial windfall bless your family.

D.1. Give yourself 1 point if True, 0 points if False. A healthy dose of independence will make you a more well-rounded and interesting person to your partner. Having all the same ideas could be boring or controlling. (See D.6.)

D.2. Give yourself 0 points if True, 1 point if False. Holding hands, sharing the good times as well as the bad, connecting on a feeling level, with no hidden agendas—being fully there in spirit as well as in person—that's what is in view here.

D.3. Give yourself 1 point if True, 0 points if False. Intentional, high-quality, interactive activities are in view here. Love is spelled T-I-M-E. Just as playtime contributed to your romance before you married, so also to your romance after marriage. Taken to extremes (see D.6.), this can be unhealthy.

D.4. Give yourself 1 point if True, 0 points if False. Outside friendships and interests should never take priority over your marriage but serve to strengthen and enhance a healthy, balanced relationship.

D.5. Give yourself 0 points if True, 1 point if False. A vacation fight could be over money or control issues. Or it could mask a hidden agenda—fear or boredom about being alone, just the two of you, for too long. Best to discuss all possibilities, then agree on a consensus solution, even one with trade-offs.

D.6. Give yourself 0 points if True, 1 point if False. There is no virtue in doing everything together. Having some personal space is necessary for healthy interdependence. Having all the same ideas could be boring or controlling. Let there be spaces in your togetherness (see D.1. and D.3.).

E.1. Give yourself 1 point if True, 0 points if False. Marriage is hard work, but the rewards of reconciling differences are surpassed only by the resources made available by God for this purpose.

E.2. Give yourself 0 points if True, 1 point if False. The inability to confess sins to one another and the related tendency to hold grudges against the other—both patterns have troublesome root causes and many unfortunate results.

E.3. Give yourself 1 point if True, 0 points if False. Those who do not pray together are more likely to prey upon one another. It is impossible to stay angry at someone you are also praying for daily.

E.4. Give yourself 0 points if True, 1 point if False. Dropping the facade and talking about what's really happening is the hallmark of a healthy relationship.

E.5. Give yourself 0 points if True, 1 point if False. As long as you are together in your commitment to share a personal faith in God at other times and places, if not always at church, you do well. All too often, disagreements on key issues or apathy about all spiritual things will hinder marital harmony.

E.6. Give yourself 1 point if True, 0 points if False. Partners come to Bible study with different experiences and needs, but you do well to submit yourselves mutually to Scripture as the final arbiter and successful enabler of healthy marriages.

How to Score
After giving yourself zero points or one point for each answer as indicated above, add up your score and find yourself in the scale below. Rest assured this inventory is very subjective and says as much about your way of viewing the glass of water ("half empty" or "half full") as it does about the objective state of your marriage. Don't be surprised if you and your mate differ in your responses to the same statements. Also, don't let false guilt weigh you down, but use this inventory to bring conviction in your plan and goal-setting for a successful marriage.

0-7 points: You have numerous weaknesses that need work to strengthen your marriage. You might consider pastoral or other professional counseling to help you identify whatever keeps you from building a successful marriage. A group of like-minded men committed to your success could also support you in setting goals to grow in these problem areas.

8-15 points: You have more weaknesses than strengths. However, with strategic goals, an agreement to work in good faith, and a support group of like-minded men to help you apply a few more successful strategies, you will greatly strengthen your marriage.

16-23 points: You have more strengths than weaknesses, and to that extent you have a strong foundation to build on and make a good marriage even better. The odds for success are in your favor, but do not take your strengths for granted. Work on identifiable weaknesses by setting goals and drawing on the support of others.

24-30 points: You have more strengths going for you than most marriages. While you may have few things to work on to become all that you want your marriage to be, do not slack off in your good faith efforts. Keep doing what you are doing and articulate those strategies for successful marriage to the next generation. That's what this book is all about!

DEVELOPING A FAMILY MISSION STATEMENT

In developing a mission statement, you can be as elaborate or as simple as you want, given your personality, gifts and desires. Excitement will build as this mission statement makes you more proactive and keeps you from being driven by everything that happens to you. Several questions beg answers, but a worthwhile mission statement should revolve around four key questions:

1. *Who are you?* (Or, what is your present situation and role?)
2. *What's going on now in your marriage in terms of strengths and weaknesses?* (Draw insights from the inventory worksheet.)
3. *What do you intend to accomplish?* (Or, what do you want to be and become as a couple? And by when? And with what consequences?)
4. *How do you plan on getting there?* (Or, what are the opportunities? The obstacles? The resources? The principles to act on?)

With answers to the above set of questions, identify the growth areas or roles God has called you into, then three goals for each area/role, then two specific action steps for each goal and—presto—you have your rough draft of a family mission statement!

Mission Statement:
Our mission as a couple is to . . .

Growth Area or Role	Strategic Goal (Who? What?)	Action Steps (How? When? etc.)
Spiritual (as a disciple)	1.	a.
		b.
	2.	a.
		b.
	3.	a.
		b.

© 1994 E. Glenn Wagner, *Strategies for a Successful Marriage.* Limited permission granted to reproduce, see page 10.

Personal (*non-work role*)	1.	a.
		b.
	2.	a.
		b.
	3.	a.
		b.
Family (*as a parent*)	1.	a.
		b.
	2.	a.
		b.
	3.	a.
		b.
Relational (*as a spouse*)	1.	a.
		b.
	2.	a.
		b.
	3.	a.
		b.
Financial (*as a steward*)	1.	a.
		b.
	2.	a.
		b.
	3.	a.
		b.

3

COMMITMENT TO GRACE

HOW DID IT GO?

1. In groups of three or four men, debrief on the progress you
   made on last session's homework assignment. Limit this discussion to fifteen minutes so you'll have time to cover the
   rest of this session. If you find you need more time for
   debriefing, plan to meet together again after this session.

   a. How far did you get toward writing a mission statement?

      ☐ I set a date to meet with my wife.
      ☐ I got as far as filling out the inventory.
      ☐ I have already met with my wife to work on and discuss
      the inventory.
      ☐ What inventory?

   b. What is your timetable for completing the mission
      statement?

   c. Have you encountered any obstacles? If so, what are they?
      Can the group help?

THOUGHTS TO PONDER
*Commitment without reflection is fanaticism in action. But reflection
without commitment is the paralysis of all action.*
—JOHN MACKAY

"If anyone would come after me, he must deny himself and take up his cross daily and follow me."
—JESUS (LUKE 9:23)

Plans and goals are great, aren't they? However, don't be like one of my former staff members who, after he had spent hours formulating his plan and writing up his goals, then placed them in the drawer of his desk and never looked at them again until the following year.

With real planning and goal-setting comes a commitment to action, and to grace. Show me your family calendar, your appointment book, or your checkbook, and I can tell what you're most committed to. Among items you have committed the most time and money to, where does your wife rank? Have you built in any special times for just the two of you? Or is she having to compete with your other priorities?

Your wife is not some appointment on the calendar or some item in the checkbook; she needs to know of your commitment to her as an individual. In committing yourself to grow together, winning at the game of marriage, you are committing yourself to experiencing God's compelling grace, or unmerited favor. Our commitment to one another is undergirded by grace; our competition from outside interests is undercut by grace.

Commitment to Grace Holds Marriages Together
Over the years Susan and I have experienced many fun times and stress-filled times. During times of great stress, the biggest need for Susan was to know my ongoing commitment to grow with her even through the difficult times. That meant a mutual commitment to experience God's grace—grace to heal past wounds and endure things that wouldn't change, grace to mesh our disparate backgrounds and preferences, grace to share the same home and life together.

When I was a pastor, couples often came to me in crisis. Many attributed their marital difficulties to having so little in common. Likewise, I have read many books on marriage which affirm that a husband and wife must have a mutual hobby, something that they enjoy doing together. This has always intrigued me because in our marriage that simply has not been the case. Although we enjoy many things together—including music, walking and talking, attending sports games, and just being together to be together—there are so many more differences. My wife loves shopping malls and flea markets; I must confess I have little patience to wander around such places. While I love golf, Susan has no desire to pursue the game, although she has tried it. We once tried playing racquetball together; that ill-fated stint had us leaving the racquetball court for the divorce court—almost!

We've since found the basis of our relationship, one which has enabled us to grow closer together and become the best of friends. *That common denominator is our commitment to God's abundant grace.*

What is grace? Think of it like this: When God extends grace to us, He does two things. First, He treats us like quarterbacks who have won the Super Bowl, rather than—as we deserve—like klutzes who have six interceptions per game. Second, He gives us the power to play the game far better than our natural skill would allow. Grace forgives and grace empowers.

Grace invites husbands and wives to treat each other with the same grace they have received from God. It allows them to rejoice in differences rather than bemoan them. It enables couples to rejoice in all they have in common in Christ, which makes all other differences seem insignificant.

Are you committed to growing with your wife? To experiencing God's grace in your life and marriage?

God's Grace Leads Us into the Area of Forgiveness and Change

A mutual commitment to God's grace will lead you to make some happy chance discoveries about yourself and your partner. The next time you are alone with your wife, don't be surprised if grace leads you into a time of confession. "If we confess our sins, he is faithful and just and will forgive us our sins" (1 John 1:9). Confessions marked by grace may sound something like this:

> "Honey, God has dealt with me today [or this week]. I've come to realize I've been wrong in the way I . . . . [OR] At times I've been very selfish and demanding, requiring that you . . . . [OR] Lately, I haven't been very kind, such as when I . . . . [OR] I have neglected your need for . . . .

"I have confessed this to God, and I've asked the men in my group to hold me accountable to change in this area, but I need you to forgive me if I am to change."

We need to be as specific with our wives as we have been with our God. In the midst of that, don't make any rash promises or boastful projections. Without pretense or self-justification, humbly acknowledge your accountability to God, allowing Him to change you by His grace.

Competition Can Build Walls, Block Grace

Without knowing grace, we fear failure. To insulate ourselves from failures (and grace!), we build walls. Rather than dealing with and rebounding from failure by God's all-forgiving grace (Romans 5:1-2), we stubbornly and fearfully go our own way, losing at the game of life and love. While "perfect love drives out fear" (1 John 4:18), it is also true that *perfect fear drives out love.* The walls of our own making in marriage do not come down without grace experienced through confession and forgiveness.

One of the NFL's winningest head football coaches illustrates what happens when there is no commitment to grace, confession, or forgiveness. This particular coach admitted the reason he lost his marriage and lost his relationship with his children was because the only thing important to him was winning at football. What disturbed me so greatly about this set of priorities was his skewed perspective about which game to win. Why not aim to win at marriage? Why not win as a father, raising kids who win at the game of life?

Perhaps men have focused for far too long on the wrong game. Men in American culture are competitive. We need a task, a goal, something to conquer, to overcome. Why not make marriage the game to win, or the hill that we are to climb, and give glory to Christ for the victory?

Commitment to grace empowers partners who want to change their relationship for the better. Such a commitment presumes that the locus of change is internal and that the means to effect those internal changes is God's all-sufficient grace. A commitment to grace asserts "the only person you can change is yourself," and its corollary, "but for the grace of God there go I." It's not what happens to us, but how we respond to provocation and adversity, that makes the difference in successful relationships. A prior commitment to God's grace as the effective change agent is what sustains couples in crisis.

God's Grace Triumphs as the One Effective Change Agent

Imagine the opposite scenario. Without a mutual, top-priority commitment to God's all-sufficient grace, the couple in crisis will come to believe those fatalistic words: "my partner will never change." Through such a closed, dark filter, we see our partner as unchanging and unchangeable. We fail to see ways she may be changing right before our eyes—all because a failure to appropriate grace lulls us into believing "my partner will never change." We may also twist those words as a knife to wound or a straitjacket to hem in our spouse.

Believing you or your partner will never change may, in effect, deny the very change you seek. Rather than deal with the unfamiliarity of a changed partner, we prefer the familiarity of our own hell. In counseling circles, this is called codependency.

There is good news that goes unheralded in all this. To say "she'll never change" is too fatalistic for the spouse whose hope springs eternal. To say "she'll never change" is a cop-out for the spouse committed to grace, which continually offers the prospect of hope and correction. The gospel of hope and grace empowers marriages to survive and thrive. "Thanks be to God, who always leads us in triumphal procession in Christ and through us spreads everywhere the fragrance of the knowledge of him" (2 Corinthians 2:14).

I can think of nothing more triumphant and empowering than saying, "You CAN change," and its corollary messages: "Here's how . . ."; "I'm with you to support you"; and "I will uphold you in the changes God brings about in your life." When I think of all the changed men that Scripture reveals—the Saul-turned-Paul types—I see grace at work, applied to winning the game of life.

Rather than viewing your partner as a change project, or as an unchangeable boor—both are self-defeating attitudes and self-fulfilling prophecies—why not change outlooks? I invite you and your partner to reaffirm the prospective change that comes from within, by God's compelling grace. Therein lies hope.

WHAT DO YOU THINK?

2. How committed are you to working on the future success of your marriage?

☐ I want desperately for my relationship to succeed, and I will go to almost any lengths to see that it does.

☐ I want very much for my relationship to succeed, and I will do all I can to see that it does.

☐ I want very much for my relationship to succeed, but I will do my fair share (and no more) to see that it does.

☐ It would be nice if my relationship succeeded, but I can't do much more than I am doing now to help it succeed.

☐ It would be nice if my relationship succeeded, but I refuse to do any more than I am doing now to keep the relationship going.

☐ My relationship can never succeed, and there is no more that I can do to keep the relationship going.

3. What would a look at your appointment calendar or checkbook reveal about the commitments you make and keep? Where does your wife rank in that list of priorities?

4. Glenn Wagner described his own marriage as one of two best friends united by their common commitment to God's grace in Jesus Christ. Other attempts at cultivating a common hobby or sport proved short-lived, even disastrous. What do you and your partner have in common?

5. Jesus' call to discipleship may be summed up, "If anyone would come after me, he must deny himself and take up his cross daily and follow me" (Luke 9:23). In calling us to commitment, Jesus calls us to our partner and to God's grace in marriage. As with our commitment to Christ, our commitment to our wife is taken up *daily*. However sincere our commitment may have been at the outset, it must be renewed today, tomorrow . . . and the next day . . . and the next day . . . until our days are done. With the call to commitment comes the gift of grace to fulfill it; such grace cannot be stockpiled, but is given daily.

a. In your marriage, what is that "cross" you must bear daily? (Hint: It's not the "thorn-in-the-side" family member you barely put up with, but is the one burden God is calling you to carry and sacrifice for.)

b. With that cross, what blessings have you received to help you bear up?

6. How is your marriage stronger because of God's grace?

☐ A mutual commitment to God's grace has opened up new possibilities of forgiveness and change.
☐ Grace has enabled me to accept the things about myself I cannot change and to change the things I can.
☐ Grace has led me to nag less and pray more for my partner.
☐ God's amazing grace not only saved "a wretch" like me, but grace also saved our marriage from becoming "a wreck" like so many.
☐ Grace disproved those fatalistic words: "my partner will never change."
☐ Other (name it):

7. A mutual commitment to God's grace led Glenn and Susan into forgiveness, change, and becoming best friends. He then proposed a sample dialogue that models confession of sin, depends on the grace of God, admits accountability to other men, and seeks forgiveness from the offended partner. Using the statement below, make your own statement of confession, filling in the blank.

Honey, God has dealt with me today [or this week]. I've come to realize. . . .

I have confessed this to God, and I've asked the men in my group to hold me accountable to change in this area, but I need you to forgive me if I am to change.

8. As time and trust permit, roleplay the above statement of confession with the men in your group. To facilitate this exercise, huddle in twos or threes with other men, who will then cheer you on as you share the statement for real later on with your spouse. Accept the fact that we all fumble the ball and deserve to get back in the game; simply tell one other person what you want to confess and seek forgiveness for. Hold one another accountable until you each follow through on this commitment to grace. But remember, accountability without affirmation is an audit—and no one likes an IRS audit or being on the witness stand.

9. The example of the NFL head coach who was more committed to winning at football than at his marriage or at parenting set Glenn to wondering whether men have been focused on winning the wrong game in life. Ask yourself: Am I a competitive person like that coach, always bent on winning? In the game of marriage, am I losing more often than I win?

    If so, you may be a "workaholic," someone who values winning at work more than winning at marriage. To find out tentatively which you value more, take the test, "How to Tell If You're a Workaholic" (page 49). Discuss the results with the men in your group.

TRY IT AT HOME
10. Confess to your wife what you wrote for question 7 of this chapter.

11. Discuss with your wife your results of the test, "How to Tell If You're a Workaholic."

12. We have imagined life committed to the gospel of grace, and we have imagined the opposite scenario—life without a mutual, top-priority commitment to God's all-sufficient grace. We affirm that the first scenario is full of hope, while the second effectively denies hope. As you read chapter 4 in preparation for the next session, begin thinking how you typically communicate your commitment, so that your spouse knows for sure where she stands with you.

HOW TO TELL IF YOU'RE A WORKAHOLIC

Some men work very long and hard hours, not because they are workaholics, not because they are materialistic, but simply because that is their only option for earning a living and supporting a family. This worksheet on overcommitments is not meant to add guilt to your life, but rather to encourage you to be creative with the time that you have. (See also "Making Time," chapter 7.)

Other men reading this book aren't overcommitted to work, but they do have a problem with overcommitment outside of work. As James Dobson says, "Husbands and wives should constantly guard against overcommitment. Even worthwhile and enjoyable activities become damaging when they consume the last ounce of energy or the remaining free moments of the day."

Yet another group of men needs to rearrange their goals and commitments to make marriage a higher priority. These men must come to grips with their workaholic tendencies. This self-scoring quiz allows you to do that. All the statements below are worded in the affirmative, so that a predominance of True (T) answers would indicate strong workaholic tendencies. For the reasons cited above, you need help from others in interpreting a high score.

If you are blind to the dynamics of workaholism in your life, your wife and/or small group could help keep you honest by holding this quiz up to you like a mirror. You may see some tendencies you don't like. The problem of workaholism goes much deeper than mere symptom recognition, and it is beyond the scope of this book or your small group to help with deep-seated workaholism.

Your answers to these twenty questions will indicate the choices and commitments you have made which may be hindering a successful marriage. If so, change what you can now, be patient with what you can't change right away, and pray for wisdom to know the difference.

1. My work excites me—generating and consuming more of my energy—more than my marriage, my family, or anything else. T F

2. While I can charge through my work and my work gives me a charge, many days I can't seem to get going or get anything done. T F

3. I take work home with me—working right through mealtimes, past bedtime, on weekends, even on vacation. T F

4. Work is the activity I like to do best and talk about most. T F

5. I work more than forty-five hours a week. T F

6. I turn my leisure pursuits into commercial ventures. T F

7. I live and die with the outcome of my work efforts. T F

8. My family and friends expect me to arrive late to dinner or whatever, because my time is always more important for something else. T F

9. I take on extra work because I fear that others can't or won't get it done otherwise. T F

10. I regularly underestimate how long a project will take and then rush to complete it. T F

11. I believe it is okay to work long hours if I love what I'm doing. T F

12. I get impatient with people who set work priorities aside for other activities (such as family, volunteer, or stay-at-home projects). T F

13. I fear that if I don't work as hard as possible, I'll lose my job or be a failure. T F

14. When things are going well and I've met my goals, I am never content but worry about the future nonetheless. T F

15. I do most things energetically and competitively, including my play, even keeping score with my spouse. T F

16. I get irritated easily when asked to stop what I'm doing to join others in doing something else. T F

17. I've been told my preoccupation with work has hurt my marriage, my family, or my other relationships. T F

18. I think about work while praying, driving, getting ready for bed, even when others are talking or the pastor is preaching. T F

19. I bring reading materials everywhere I go, even to the table and into bed. T F

20. I believe that "making money" (from work) will solve the problems of "making time" for my spouse. T F

4

COMMUNICATION WITHIN MARRIAGE
Five Ways to Build Up Your Mate and Not Grieve the Holy Spirit

HOW DID IT GO?

1. In groups of three or four men, debrief on the progress you made on last session's homework assignment. Limit this discussion to ten minutes so you'll have time to cover the rest of this session. If you find you need more time for debriefing, plan to meet together again after this session.

   a. What happened when you confessed to your wife?

   b. What did you learn from the test on workaholism? Is there any action you need to take?

THOUGHTS TO PONDER

[25]*Therefore each of you must put off falsehood and speak truthfully to his neighbor, for we are all members of one body.* [26]*"In your anger do not sin": Do not let the sun go down while you are still angry,* [27]*and do not give the devil a foothold. . . .*

[29]*Do not let any unwholesome talk come out of your mouths, but only what is helpful for building others up according to their needs, that it may benefit those who listen.* [30]*And do not grieve the Holy Spirit of God, with whom you were sealed for the day of redemption.* [31]*Get rid of all bitterness, rage and anger, brawling and slander, along with every form of malice.* [32]*Be kind and compassionate to one another, forgiving each other, just as in Christ God forgave you.*

—THE APOSTLE PAUL (EPHESIANS 4:25-32)

Knowing when to say nothing is 50 percent of tact and 90 percent of marriage.
   —SYDNEY J. HARRIS

The literal sense of the Greek in Ephesians 4:30 reads, "*Stop grieving* the Holy Spirit." Paul assumes that grieving the Spirit is our natural or habitual tendency. If left to ourselves, we would continue to bring grief or pain to the heart of God.

Peter caused and felt this kind of grief when he betrayed the Lord Jesus (Luke 22:54-62). The Lord felt the same as He wept over Jerusalem (Luke 19:41) and over Lazarus (John 11:35-36). We all experience this broken-hearted grief when someone we love wounds or disappoints us deeply.

The way we communicate within marriage often brings pain to God's heart, as well as to the heart of the one we say we love. However, we can build up our mate and stop grieving God by learning to communicate effectively within marriage. Five principles of good communication are outlined in Ephesians 4:25-32.

Stop Lying and Start Telling the Truth (Ephesians 4:25)
Unfortunately, lying has become a national pastime. We begin to believe that everyone lies if it's in his or her best interest, so what's the harm in a little cover-up? If my wife isn't the wiser, why not a little lie or half-truth that protects the status quo? After all, if it avoids conflict or a hassle, we're much better off, right?

Wrong! Paul says, "Put off falsehood." The construction of the verb in the original Greek means you, and only you, can put it off, or set it aside. We are called to halt all forms and degrees of lying. "Wait a minute," you may be saying. "I don't lie to my wife, and my wife does not lie to me." If that's what you think, put yourself in this scenario:

You had a bad day at work. You're frustrated and troubled by what took place, but you really don't want to talk about it with anyone at home. When you arrive there, the kids greet you at the door, but you slide them aside after grunting, "Hello." Your wife beams at you, embracing you with a warm hug and sweet kiss. But you respond like a palm tree stiffly letting the breeze go by.

To her acute emotional sensors, something smells fishy. So she pulls you aside and asks, "Honey, what's wrong?" You reply,

"Oh, nothing." She persists because she knows you so well, "But Honey, it seems something is wrong. What is it?" Again you discount her perceptions by saying, "Nothing." She tries one more time. You reply, "Nothing is wrong, but if you continue to bug me, something will really be wrong." You storm off to the other room.

Everyone in that scenario knows you've lied. Would it not have been easier—and more truthful—to say, "Honey, some problems at work are bothering me, but I don't feel free to talk about them right now. If you give me some time later, I'll let you know what's going down, because I know you want to help me work through it. You are a vital part of my life, but now is not the right time for discussion."

Building a successful marriage means learning to speak the truth, as difficult or inconvenient as that may be at times. Of course, this does not mean that we do so in anger or without tact.

Be Angry Without Sinning (Ephesians 4:26)

Paul's admonition—"Be angry, but don't sin"—may sound strange to people used to hearing, "Don't worry, be happy." I believe God gives us the emotion of anger, not to attack or destroy people, but rather to attack a problem. Herein lies our difficulty. As Aristotle said, "Anybody can become angry—that is easy. But to be angry with the right person, and to the right degree, and at the right time, and for the right purpose, and in the right way—that is not within everybody's power."

Apparently, we can be angry without sinning. But he who is angry "without sinning" had best be angry *at sin*—and sin alone—not the sinner. Several New Testament words translate the idea of rage or anger. One has the idea of a violent outburst, one that flies off the handle. (We all know what happens to someone who flies off in a rage—he has a very bad landing.) People who are this angry should take a lesson from flight technicians: count down before blasting off. God displays this kind of angry outburst in His fury against sin, but this New Testament word is never used in a good context when referring to Christians.

Another New Testament word for anger conveys a subtle and settled disposition of mind. Such anger does not flare up but burns long and slow. That's the word Paul uses here (Ephesians

4:26), which suggests that the anger we feel toward a particular problem or sin has a settled disposition or rational basis. At times we should be angry—not violently flying off the handle—but mad enough to do something about the social injustice, the unfair situation, or whatever the problem is.

If we can't get angry at sin, then there is something wrong with us as believers. However, getting angry at a *person* is always wrong. That distinction between "hating the sin" but "loving the sinner" is tough to make in actual practice. Those who do successfully make this distinction are full of passion for justice—to right the wrong—yet overflowing with mercy—to restore the wrongdoer. Abraham Lincoln comes to mind as an exemplar of this dual ethic. He declared war against the evil institutions of slavery, yet exhibited "malice toward none" after the bloody Civil War.

Avoid Meltdown or "BUBUs"—Letting Anger Build Up and Blow Up

Don't give the devil a foothold (Ephesians 4:26-27). Keep short accounts—empty your backpack of anger before the day's end. Otherwise, if you let anger build up, it will blow up. That's what Paul means by urging us, "Do not let the sun go down while you are still angry" (Ephesians 4:26).

That does not mean we badger our spouse into staying awake until the problem is resolved. That's another form of abuse and diverts attention from the presenting problem. Nor does "not letting the sun go down" mean we cannot allow ourselves sleep until the situation is resolved. Some couples wear themselves out and exacerbate the problem trying to resolve it before bedtime. What they don't understand is that the more they postpone sleep, growing more tired and irritable, the more elusive the solution becomes.

However, you can and should deal with built-up anger before nodding off to sleep. Seize the moment to seek forgiveness, reconciliation, and restoration. Set a time when you are well-rested in which to deal with the problem. Reassure your wife (and yourself) that you are not attacking her, but rather the problem. By making sure your relationship is right, you have doubled the resources for tackling the unresolved problem.

To make sure your relationship is right, you must respond

COMMUNICATION WITHIN MARRIAGE 55

immediately to wrongful, hurtful, misdirected anger—whether displayed by yourself or your wife. When sinful anger first raises its ugly head against another person, especially against your spouse, that's when you slay it, confess it, and regain control. Name it and tame it. If you don't confess it, to yourself and to God, your anger will build up and spill out at the most inopportune times.

I can hear a cry of protest: "But you don't know what my wife did to me!" Or, "You don't understand all the pain I've had to bear." You're right, I don't. But when I get that angry, I am reminded of the Chinese proverb: "I was angry, for I had no shoes. Then I met a man who had no feet."

I am also reminded of our Lord Jesus and the need to place myself in His shoes. He suffered far more miscarriage of justice than we ever will, even the sham of a trial and the shame of the cross (Mark 14:53–15:32, Hebrews 12:1-4). Jesus confronted sin and restrained evil head on, but not once did He retaliate with hateful speech or threaten personal revenge, even when tempted and capable of doing so.

You have the attitude of Christ within you (Philippians 2:5). That helps you do as Jesus would in such anger-producing situations. When we do not think and react like Jesus, this grieves the Holy Spirit and brings pain to God's heart.

While we should not become or stay angry at our spouse, anger is perfectly understandable and manageable—if dealt with immediately. This is easier said than done. Suppose you had a "disagreement" (euphemism for "heated argument"), with no immediate resolution in sight before going to bed. You're lying there restless, unable to sleep. You know the problem ought to be solved, but you stubbornly wait for her to take the initiative. You're thinking to yourself, *All my wife needs to do, for me to get some sleep tonight, is just roll over, put her hand on my shoulder, and apologize; then we'll be okay.*

Simultaneously she's thinking to herself, *If this lug beside me would just once have enough humility to admit when he is wrong, to roll over and lovingly embrace me, I would forgive him in a moment; then I could get some great sleep tonight.*

Instead, you both lie there—sleepless in anger—forgoing the blessed sleep you could have enjoyed, if only you had humbled yourself and taken the initiative.

Perhaps being "sleepless in anger" hasn't happened to you, but it happened to me and it happens to many other men I know. If you should find yourself going to bed still angry, respond immediately. Otherwise, bitterness and resentment begin to well up within the heart. Worse yet, the devil will get a foothold. He will bait and entice a person who has bitterness in his heart. Be wise to such wiles of the devil; don't give him any platform by which he can make further inroads into your marriage.

Embrace the good news: *Confessing anger keeps bitterness from taking root and becoming hatred.* Anger is only a weed, easily uprooted, but hatred is the tree, hard to chop down. When you deal with the anger promptly and properly, you remove that opportunity for the devil to grow a tree of hate and tempt you in other areas. Without a foothold, the devil cannot fracture your marriage.

Speak Words of Edification (Ephesians 4:29)
When Paul says, "Do not let any unwholesome talk come out of your mouths" (Ephesians 4:29), he has in mind those cutting, slicing, nasty remarks we learned as kids and perfected as adults. Those childish putdowns, said in jest or in haste, we wish we could recall as soon as we say them. As children we learned to say, "Sticks and stones may break my bones, but names will never hurt me." But as adults we know the opposite is true. Words do penetrate and spread—for good or for evil. "Reckless words pierce like a sword, but the tongue of the wise brings healing" (Proverbs 12:18).

Words have power to wound or heal because what is done *in* you is far more damaging than what is done *to* you. "The words of a gossip are like choice morsels; they go down to a man's inmost parts" (Proverbs 18:8). To respond to one cutting remark with another one is like trying to clean up dirt with mud. Real communication stops, and personal attack takes over. We have two ways to speak the truth: one which tears down and a second which builds up.

Sometimes we tear down in a joking manner. Never, under any circumstance, should you speak down to your wife, not even in jest, and especially not in public. When we ridicule, everyone laughs on the outside, but pain seeps into the heart. Nasty remarks have a way of settling into her heart deeper than all our kind intentions.

Speak the truth in love to help her grow—in relationship to Christ and in relationship to you. In each situation, you have a choice to make: words that build, or words that destroy.

This point was driven home to me by a pastor-friend of mine who found himself in a sticky situation. When the pastor's wife fell ill, a member of his church went out of her way to prepare a very special recipe for the pastor's family. But when they sat down to dinner, no one would eat it. Instead, the family went to a fast-food restaurant. The pastor then had to decide what to say to the lady who provided the neglected meal. He thought long and hard about speaking the truth in love and when the appointed time arrived, he had his answer. When she came by, she popped the inevitable question with much enthusiasm, "How did you like the dinner that I prepared? It was my late husband's favorite recipe."

Aha, so that's what killed him, he said—to himself, not to her. With a smile, handing her the dishes, he said in truth, "All I can tell you is that food like this doesn't last long around our house." She became exuberant, skipping away. Such tactfulness, or choosing words carefully, is part of telling the truth in love and brings healing rather than hurt.

Our words should not only avoid doing harm but should intentionally build up the other person. Look for the good and praise your wife for it. For example, praise her when she handles a crisis well.

Edifying, wholesome speech doesn't preclude rebuking or confronting someone about offensive behavior. Yet even such true talk or tough love should not be conveyed with a hard edge or harsh attitude. A friend of mine in college had a habit of telling the truth in a way or context that felt like daggers twisted into the heart by a foe. "Wounds from a friend can be trusted, but an enemy multiplies kisses" (Proverbs 27:6). Or, as the late Francis Shaeffer was fond of saying, "If we cannot confront with tears in our eyes, then we are confronting in an unbiblical manner."

If your speech is not especially loving or edifying, then repentance and forgiveness are in order.

Forgiveness Covers a Multitude of Sins

Forgiving one another will cover a multitude of problems and difficulties within your marriage. "Love is blind," they say, concurring with the Apostle Paul that love does not keep track of wrongdoing (1 Corinthians 13:5). However, love is also true talk, honest feelings, and realistic consequences. We are to think and listen twice before we speak even once. (That's why we have two ears and only one mouth.)

When Susan and I were first married, we lived on a Florida estate where we served as domestic help. Our apartment was thirteen by fifteen feet—which included living room, dining room, bedroom, and kitchen. The couple we served modeled valuable lessons in communication—not all positive.

This couple, despite their wealth, were poverty-stricken communicators. The lady of the house was hard of hearing, a problem further complicated when she deliberately turned off her hearing aid. The hearing aid remained off whenever she had large amounts of information to dump on her husband. Without her tuning in, he could not get a word in edgewise, no matter how loud he shouted.

This led to some great sideshows for Susan and me, though I'm not sure the husband was amused by it all. Once he blasted her with the air horn taken from his boat, all the while shouting at her to turn on her hearing aid. However, even that piercing horn blast could not get through. Later, when the conversation wasn't so heated, he simply lifted his hand to stop her talking long enough so he could communicate with her. The lifted hand worked, whereas the air horn did not.

From their hilarious (but painful) sideshow, I actually learned a good communication strategy for couples. If either partner notices that communication has ceased and character assassination has begun, he or she has the right and obligation simply to lift a hand to stop all talking. The raised hand is like a referee's irrevocable timeout call. It says, "We need to break in, back up, start over, perhaps even take a timeout for cooling off." Raised hands can lead to holding hands, as you restore your relationship and attack the problem—the contested issue and the vested interests—not the personalities.

The raised-hand technique backs up what the Apostle James said, "Everyone should be quick to listen, slow to speak and slow to become angry" (James 1:19). "Quick to listen" means quick to forgive—"just as in Christ God forgave you" (Ephesians 4:32). Such quickness in forgiveness applies to our extending, as well as asking for, forgiveness.

When Susan and I have disagreed on issues over the years, I've been amazed and humbled at how often she has been right and I have been wrong. Her opinion, wisdom, intuition, and even emotional response to some scenario often proves insightful and trustworthy, whereas I can be totally clueless in my thinking. I've learned to affirm her gifts in this area.

Men, let your wife know you value her for this vital role she plays. The macho idea that men must make all the decisions, or have the final say, is not what marriage is about. Marriage is about a vibrant partnership, two coming together as one—and those two submerging their wills and living for the glory of God. When we forgive our partner, God opens up avenues for communication. Saying, "Maybe you're right" or "I was wrong" opens up communication more than anything I know. Ask God to make your words sweet, and He will do so with the love of Christ. The love of Christ for the Church demonstrates a husband's love for his wife, and vice versa, as we learn in the next chapter.

WHAT DO YOU THINK?

2. As we warned about bad communication patterns that grieve the Holy Spirit, what was going through your mind?

☐ Whew! Thank God they weren't talking about me.

☐ Ouch! Stop hitting so close to home.

☐ Help! I get angry in all the wrong ways and I can't seem to stop.

☐ I may have blown up only once or twice a year, but I am still dealing with the fallout from those explosions.

☐ I have trouble reading the symptoms that indicate when I am getting angry; this chapter raised key issues I will explore further.

☐ Wagner and Gruen blew the whole issue of anger out of proportion to the actual problem.

☐ I lost sleep just thinking about being "sleepless in anger."

☐ I yearn to teach my children about anger management and edifying speech, especially given the poor communication models I've grown up with.

3. Put yourself in Glenn's all-too-familiar scenario of the husband who lied when asked, "Honey, what's wrong?" If that were you who had just lied, what would be your reason?

☐ The truth is too painful or difficult to express.
☐ I'm afraid of conflict.
☐ The timing is wrong.
☐ I always have trouble expressing my true feelings.
☐ Other (name it):

4. Put yourself in the other scenario of the husband and wife lying "sleepless in anger."

   a. When this happens in your marriage, who usually initiates a confession of anger and resolution of the problem, to avoid a "BUBU" (Building Up and Blowing Up)?

   b. In what relationships have you seen a "tree of hate" grow from a "weed of anger" that was not quickly uprooted?

5. Certain clue words indicate when we are lacing our speech with zingers or "unwholesome talk" (Ephesians 4:29). The number of hurtful words is endless, but here are a few to be aware of. Which ones do you think you use?
   Feel free to add to this starter list. Then covenant with your small group and your spouse to "never again" use any words from this list in a hurtful way, especially with your spouse.

☐ "You *always* . . ." or "You *never*. . . ."
☐ Unkind comparisons: "If only you were a good wife or mother like so-and-so. . . ."
☐ Unfair accusations, ridicule, or particular "hot buttons."
☐ Blame-shifting and bringing up the past.
☐ Any degrading, demeaning, sexist, or vulgar names (even in jest).
☐ Other (name them):

6. Look back at Ephesians 4:25-32 (page 51).

   a. Since your wife is your nearest "neighbor" (4:25), how should you speak to her?

   b. How is it possible to be angry "without sinning"?

   c. How is it possible to be angry at sin but not sinners?

   d. Is Paul saying here, "If you don't have anything nice to say, don't say anything at all"? Explain.

   e. If love does not keep track of wrongdoing (1 Corinthians 13:5), is Paul then saying, "Love means never having to say you're sorry"? Explain.

7. Men have a habit of building some small but effective barriers to communication. Which of these have you built?

   ☐ I've been so concerned about getting my opinion across that my spouse can't get a word in edgewise.
   ☐ I become irritated at the slow rate of speed with which my wife is speaking, so I jump in and finish her sentences.
   ☐ I'm concerned only with the punch line and not all her details, so I fill in the gaps, hasten the story along, or steal her thunder.
   ☐ I disengage myself by letting my wife do all the talking for me.
   ☐ I exaggerate for dramatic effect, turning molehills into mountains, when only the facts were called for.
   ☐ I save face, sidetrack the issue, or shift blame away from me.
   ☐ I'm unwilling to drop what I'm engaged in and actively listen to my wife's feelings. Instead, I try to "fix it."
   ☐ I may hear what she says, but not what she means.

8. Have you had any recent success in breaking down any of those communication barriers, or others? Which ones?

9. (*Optional*) Try an experiment with "active listening." Active listening means not just sitting and passively letting someone's words wash over you, but rather actively trying to absorb what he or she is saying. Since most of us are poor to average at active listening, this exercise gives you a chance to practice with the other men in your group. Play three rounds, fifteen minutes total.

   Break up into groups of three. Person A will recount a personal story about telling a "white lie" to his wife, lying awake angry in bed, or building one of the barriers listed in question 7. Person B will try to listen actively to the story.

   Person C will judge the quality of the listening and monitor the clock. After three minutes of listening without interruption, Person B will reflect back in paraphrased form what he heard Person A say, being careful to accurately reflect all statements of feeling and meaning. Allow one minute for this paraphrased feedback, then allow Person A to confirm that this indeed was what he intended. If Person B got it wrong, repeat the procedure for one more minute until he gets it right.

   When the five minutes are up, rotate roles, so that Person A is actively listening and giving feedback to Person C, who then confirms the feedback, with Person B observing the conversation and the clock.

   After this second five-minute round, rotate roles one last time. In this third and final round, Person C is actively listening to Person B, with Person A observing the conversation and the clock for five minutes.

   The goal of this exercise is to build up your listening skills so that you can build up your mate. Along the way, you will have enjoyed getting to know two men in your group, as you swap stories and try to listen and translate the feelings and meanings involved.

TRY IT AT HOME
10. Whole books and seminars in marriage enrichment expand on this strategy of good communication. We have barely

introduced some of the barriers to communication and the ways that successful marriages overcome those barriers. In future weeks, make a point of checking in with one another to find out how communication is going on the home front.

11. Try actively listening to your wife this week. Do you catch yourself building one of the barriers to communication?

12. Make two photocopies of the "Romance Check-In" on pages 76-78 for use with this study (see page 10). Bring one copy with you to your next group meeting, when you discuss chapter 5. You'll fill in that copy along with your group. Afterward, you'll give the other copy to your wife to fill in. (*Warning:* You might not want to let her see it until after you've had a chance to work through it.)

13. As you read chapter 5 in preparation for the next session, begin thinking of the different languages of love you and your wife speak. Sometimes we are very selective in the ways we send or receive messages of love; often our partners are not tuned into that frequency. When that happens, our efforts to show love fall on deaf ears. More about that in the next chapter.

5

LOVING YOUR MATE WITH THE LOVE OF CHRIST
Because God in Christ Has Romanced Us to Himself

HOW DID IT GO?
1. Did you have any success with active listening this week? Take no more than ten minutes to report on how it went.

THOUGHTS TO PONDER
Love is not the cause of good relationships, it is the consequence of good relationships. . . . Love is seldom spontaneous, instant, dynamic. It usually takes considerable time to create. It results from work, from thinking, from promoting equality, from being able to cope and adapt.
—WILLIAM LEDERER

You learn to speak by speaking, to study by studying, to run by running, to work by working; and just so you learn to love God and man by loving. Begin as a mere apprentice, and the very power of love will lead you on to become a master of the art.
—SAINT FRANCIS OF SALES (1567–1622)

[16]*This is how we know what love is: Jesus Christ laid down his life for us. And we ought to lay down our lives for our brothers.* [17]*If anyone has material possessions and sees his brother in need but has no pity on him, how can the love of God be in him?* [18]*Dear children, let us not love with words or tongue but with actions and in truth. . . .*
[7]*Dear friends, let us love one another, for love comes from God. Everyone who loves has been born of God and knows God.* [8]*Whoever does not love does not know God, because God is love.* [9]*This is how God showed his love among us: He sent his one and only Son into the world that we might live through him.* [10]*This is*

love: not that we loved God, but that he loved us and sent his Son as an atoning sacrifice for our sins.
—THE APOSTLE JOHN (1 JOHN 3:16-18, 4:7-10)

The Greek language has four different words for love, describing the many dimensions of loving relationships:

- The first word, *storgé*, conveys the idea of fondness, devotion, or connectedness within a family, as in Romans 12:10.
- *Eros* connotes physical intimacy or sexual love. We have no New Testament uses of this word.
- *Phileo* is Greek for companionship love or friendship. To Jesus, the twelve disciples were His *friends*, not His servants (John 15:13-15). *Phileo* is the strong measure of Jesus' love for Lazarus (John 11:3,36), God's love for Jesus' disciples (John 16:27), Peter's love for Jesus (John 21:15-17), even Judas' "kiss" of Jesus (Matthew 26:48). So also *phileo* characterizes strong marriages, which are between best friends and true companions, not masters and servants.
- However, the kind of love most needed within our marriages is *agape* love, which may be defined as unconditional positive regard, a profound concern for the well-being of another, or love-in-action-with-no-strings-attached. *Agape* characterized Jesus' love of Peter, even if Peter could muster only *phileo* for Jesus (John 21:15-21). Christ loved the church with *agape* (1 John 4:7-10), so that husbands would love their wives likewise (Ephesians 5:25). This *agape* love that radiates from God is reflected in a husband's love for his wife.

Loving Our Mate Is Compelled by *God's Prior Love for Us*
God is the source of agape love (1 John 4:7). A growing relationship with my God will result in a growing ability to love my wife with His love. God's love pours into our hearts by the Holy Spirit (Romans 5:5), who produces the spiritual fruit of love in me (Galatians 5:22-23). God's nature and purpose is love (1 John 4:8,16). To the extent that the very nature of God is completed in us (1 John 4:12), we have His love for others. And vice versa—love for one another reflects and perfects the love of God in us (1 John 4:12,17,20).

Loving Our Mate with God's Love Involves *No Strings Attached*

God's love is delivered to us and through us without demanding readiness or reciprocity on our part. There's nothing we can do to make God stop loving us. And with God's initiating love compelling us (1 John 4:10,19), we love our wives. God doesn't wait for us to be loving before He loves, so why should we wait for our wives to come around? God does not base His love on whether or not I'm lovely or even lovable (Romans 5:6-8), but only on the fact that it is His nature to love.

Once I understand and appreciate agape love, I am compelled to reflect it more fully in my marriage. God's love compels me to give without thought of what I'll receive in return. Yet we husbands tend to believe, subconsciously, that our wives do not notice, appreciate or deserve how much we do for them. When we remind them how indebted they are to us, we are controlling and manipulating, not loving, our wives.

Men, we can't fool our wives; they know from experience and a sixth sense when we demand a reciprocal love, in which case the love of God is not in us.

Loving Our Mate with God's Love Involves *an Explicit Action*

Men are known to say, "Honey, I do love you. Just because I don't show it doesn't mean I don't love you." To such an attitude the Apostle John responds, "Dear children, let us not love with words or tongue but with actions and in truth" (1 John 3:18).

We husbands tend to believe love is demonstrated by our hard work, bringing home the paycheck, or in the vacations and other activities we plan on a grand scale. But our wives are looking for the little things. Doing errands and chores we don't like—the ones posted by the refrigerator or phone—if done without a beef but with a cheerful attitude, our partners will interpret as love.

Once, when Susan had been working many long hours at her job, things around the house simply were not getting done. So I arranged with the children to help out, along with friends of mine who worked for a cleaning company, to do the house from top to bottom. We made it a family project in order to encourage Susan. The only difficulty was when she arrived home before everyone could clear out; no matter, we simply "kidnapped" a tired Susan until all was completed. Then we "knocked her out" with a job well done.

Ever try telling your wife, "Give me a list of the things you want done this weekend, and I'll see that they're accomplished"? After you help her regain consciousness and composure, you can follow through on your shocking intentions.

Loving Our Mate with God's Love Involves *Sacrificial Giving*
Love thinks of giving, not getting. While it is possible to give without loving, you cannot love without giving. Love never calculates what's in this for me, except in a special sense: With love, unlike with money, the more you give it away, the more it multiplies and comes back to you.

I often counsel young couples who describe their marriages as a fifty-fifty, give-and-take proposition. Each spouse divides the work and takes responsibility for doing his or her fair share, and only their fair share; they meet the other one halfway, and go no further.

I have been quick (and tactful) to tell them that they are wrong. Marriage is 100 percent my giving to my wife what she needs and fulfilling the responsibilities that God has placed on me. Marriage is also 100 percent her responsibility to give to me and freely make the sacrifices that God calls her to make. Sacrificial service for the other's well-being, or agape love, doesn't mean going halfway—it's more like "all-out." God did not hold back, coming just halfway to earth or going halfway to the cross. Rather "God *so loved* the world that He *gave* His only Son" (John 3:16). That is, God in Christ *romanced* us to Himself.

Let us go and do likewise, and love with all that He has given us. Many men understand this in a macho sense, especially around Valentine's Day, acknowledging their willingness to "die" for their one-and-only. I don't doubt the sincerity of such professions of love. However, the more difficult calling for husbands who are not martyrs is this: *living* sacrificially for her *day to day*. That may be more difficult than *dying* sacrificially by giving your life's blood in one heroic moment. To live sacrificially for your wife is to set your goals and ambitions aside to pursue the needs of her heart. This means discerning what she wants and then subjugating your desires to hers.

Loving Our Mate with the Love of Christ Involves Forgiveness

Jesus Christ has forgiven you for all that you've done—totally and completely. Aren't you happy for that good news? Doesn't that make you want to treat your wife in the same way? We are to forgive as we have been forgiven (Ephesians 4:32).

I remember speaking with a man whose wife had walked out on him. Over a period of time she decided she wanted back in—to give the marriage a good second chance. His response was casual and conditional: "I'll take her back and see if this works out, but I'm not going to forgive her yet. I don't think I can do that."

Taken aback by his comment, I asked him for permission to say something about forgiveness: "As long as you are unwilling to forgive her, your marriage will not work. It doesn't matter whether your wife is meeting all of your expectations or not. If you cannot offer the forgiveness of Christ, then the wall between you will remain."

Loving Our Mate with the Love of Christ Involves Complete Acceptance

Christ views us as holy and blameless—"without stain or wrinkle or any other blemish" (Ephesians 5:27). That is, we are accepted totally, without reservation. God wants men to view their wives "without a wrinkle," that is, without a fault. There is no greater need among wives than to know their husbands accept them—unconditionally—no matter how they look or cook, how they walk or talk, or how many wrinkles, layers, or pounds they have gained.

A man I know called off his wedding when his fiancée regained the forty-five pounds she had taken off prior to their engagement. He felt defrauded, and she felt only his conditional love. She was right. When he realized his love for her was only conditional on keeping the weight off, they wisely put off the wedding until he, or another suitor, could love her unconditionally. Fourteen months after the initial wedding date was called off, he still could not bring himself to drop the standards he held for his fiancée. Today she is happily married to someone else who loves her unconditionally.

A recent study of women who work outside their home

revealed that they receive a great measure of esteem from their jobs and their reception in the marketplace. Yet the same studies have shown that, if the working woman is married, her husband's attitude toward her affects her sense of well-being much more than her career. If a woman does not feel accepted and loved by her husband, no amount of success in other venues can make up for that sense of loss.

Loving Our Mate with the Love of Christ Involves *Commitment*

Your wife needs to know you've made a commitment to her. However, your profession of love cannot be purely financial; her love cannot be bought, as Solomon's beloved woman (Song of Songs 8:6-7) confesses:

> Place me like a seal over your heart,
>   like a seal on your arm;
> for love is as strong as death,
>   its jealousy [ardor] as unyielding as the grave.
> It burns like blazing fire,
>   like a mighty flame.
> Many waters cannot quench love;
>   rivers cannot wash it away.
> If one were to give all the wealth of his house for love,
>   it would be utterly scorned.

They say "diamonds are forever." Maybe so, but romantic love is ephemeral. People marry out of love but don't stay married if they fall out of love. Divorce is a testimony not so much to the failure of love, as to the inability and unwillingness of people to live without love. Love doesn't fail; people do. Love may be like a fire, but that all-consuming fire needs a fireplace—a place to call its own, lest it spread like wildfire to every tree.

God intended that "a man leaves his father and his mother and cleaves to his wife, and they become one flesh" (Genesis 2:24, Ephesians 5:31; RSV). Marriage entails leaving parents and forsaking all other loves—including self-love. As Ben Franklin once said, "He that falls in love with himself will have no rivals." In this respect, a successful marriage requires an emotional, as well as physical leave-taking. You and I cannot be stuck on ourselves or stuck to our parents if we are to stick to our wife and enjoy intimacy in marriage.

The old-fashioned word *cleave* conveys the idea of gluing or joining yourself to your wife in total commitment. Two pieces of paper solidly glued together create one super-strength piece that cannot be separated again along the seam; the new creation can only be torn crosswise. Likewise, take two blocks of brick or stone, put mortar between them, allow to dry, and they are stuck—impossible to pull apart. Try telling your wife (with a wink), "You're stuck with me." Or try, "I'm stuck on you!" Or, better yet, "Nothing can pull us apart."

I can just hear some comics turning that first phrase around, saying, "You bet I'm stuck with her." Resist the temptation to cynicism. Be a man who actively and unashamedly glues himself to his wife. Let your wife know you are completely committed to her. God puts this responsibility for stick-to-itiveness upon the husband. Many women get their hearts broken and their spirits crushed because the husband simply fails to affirm, and reaffirm, his commitment to her.

Conversely, one promise keeper I know made himself vulnerable to his troubled, tearful wife, saying to her, "No matter what action you take [to divorce], I will never leave you or forsake you." Disarmed and buoyed by his non-retaliatory, unconditional commitment to her, she backed down.

Loving Our Mate with the Love of Christ Involves *Praise*
Practice telling your wife you love her on a daily basis (Proverbs 31:28). Praise motivates and shows value. Praise her publicly. Praise her privately. Praise her in front of the family. Be creative in your praise. Instead of general praise ("You're a great wife"), offer specific observations. For example, say, "I appreciate you for the way you. . . . I praise God for giving me a wife such as you."

The British statesmen Winston Churchill was renowned as a loving and committed husband. When dozens of dignitaries at a formal banquet in London were each, in turn, asked, "If you could not be who you are, who would you like to be?" all eyes were on Churchill. He did not disappoint. "If I could not be who I am, I would most like to be. . . ." At this point he paused, teased out the suspenseful moment, reached for the hand of his wife, the beloved Clementine, and then continued—"Lady

Churchill's *second* husband."

What a way to make points with your wife! His comments apply to anyone who wants to build a successful marriage.

The bottom line, summing up all eight ways of showing love to our mates, is this: *Our wife's needs are best met with the compassion of Christ.*

WHAT DO YOU THINK?

2. Women have described their husbands in various terms. Which of their answers interests you, or applies to you?

☐ The hard-working, Type A personality: "Honey, I love you, but I have so much to do, so much money to make, so little time to do it."

☐ The stuck-on-himself, narcissistic type: "I love you but I have needs, too, and they are more important. I'm more needy than you are."

☐ The macho husband, after an hour of primping in the mirror or pumping iron: "Don't you just love my body?"

☐ The stop-spending-my-money, cheapskate kind of husband: "All you want me around for is my money, and I want you to stop spending it." (He buys every toy he wants; she gets an allowance for groceries.)

☐ The conceited, controlling husband: "You don't deserve a man like me," to which one wife replied, "I don't deserve migraine headaches, either, but I've still got them."

☐ The boorish husband whose wife said, "We need more romance," to which he replied, "No, Honey, we need *less* romance."

☐ The other-centered husband: "Sweetheart, you've been carrying quite a load lately. How can I help?"

3. Most men associate loving their wives with sexual intimacy. While Scripture does command husbands not to deprive their wives sexually (1 Corinthians 7:3-5), it is even more important to love our wives *sacrificially*—with *agape* or the love of Jesus Christ.

a. What big difference do you see between the two kinds of love—*eros* and *agape*?

b. Would you love your wife any differently if you romanced her with the same love of God, *agape*, with which Christ romances you (1 John 4:19)? Explain.

c. In the context of mutual submission (Ephesians 5:21) and following the pattern of Christ (5:25), how does a husband submit to his wife? (*Hint:* When did we see Christ submit to His bride, the Church?)

4. The biblical principle of sacrificial service or unbridled giving is modeled for us and compelled in us by the love of Christ for the Church (Ephesians 5:21-33, 1 John 4:7-10). To make this practical, put yourself in this scenario from Glenn's life:

Susan and I moved around a lot and did not always have our own home. She has this incredible knack of making whatever humble abode we're staying in feel like home. Recently we moved into a new house, with much stress and difficulty, complicated by holiday company moving in right on top of us. This unsettledness had been going on for weeks, when I came home one day to discover all her "country clutter," as I like to call it, neatly displayed on the walls—no thanks to me. What she had made or purchased over the years she carried from place to place, and these decorations transformed any place into our home.

I rebuked myself for not putting her first. I should have noticed that the unsettledness at home was adding to her stress and made it a priority to help her decorate the house. In failing to notice her needs and meet them, I missed a golden opportunity to express the love I have for her.

When did you last miss a similar golden opportunity to express the love you have for your wife?

5. In our story of the two suitors, the second suitor loved unconditionally, while the first could not completely accept his fiancée with forty-five extra pounds. Many men are more concerned about their wife's gaining weight than about their

own fitness. Ask yourself: Am I more like the first or the second suitor? How so, or in what situations? Where (else) might I have a double standard—one for me, one for her—which is less than completely accepting?

6. a. Complete the worksheet, "Romance Check-In" (pages 76-78), on your own, now, within the allotted time for your group. After completing this worksheet, meet in groups of four to discuss your reactions. Doing this with other men should be fun—because it is so uncomfortable. A man can be married fifteen to twenty years and still not know the little things that demonstrate he really loves his wife.

   b. Ask yourself: Did I find myself making excuses or jokes about not dating my mate? Any excuses like these:

   ☐ This would never work in a family with little children.
   ☐ We don't have the money for many of those dating ideas.
   ☐ We may have the money, but in a two-income family, who has time?
   ☐ We may have the money and the time, but who has the energy?
   ☐ We may have the money, the time, and the energy, but in our town there's nothing to do but watch the grass grow.
   ☐ These dating ideas are so much fun, I'd feel like I was having an "affair" with my wife if I sneaked a "date" onto our weekly calendar.
   ☐ We're married, so you don't expect us to keep on dating, do you?
   ☐ I've run out of excuses but, to be frank, I've also lost the romantic spark.

TRY IT AT HOME
   7. Ask your wife to complete her own blank copy of the "Romance Check-In." Then compare notes and make dates together. But beware of what might happen if she gets hold

of this "Romance Check-In" before you do. Who knows? You might even begin dating your mate and get to know her all over again! What goes around comes around.

8. Speaking of fun, the "Romance Check-In" is also meant to prime the pump for chapter 6 on romance and fun. As you read chapter 6 in preparation for the next session, begin thinking of even more ways you might rekindle the romance and redouble the fun in building a successful marriage together.

When you meet to discuss chapter 6, you'll each need a Bible because you'll be examining the Song of Songs, a romantic love poem written to celebrate a marriage. Also, the group leader should be prepared to model his own response to question 5 of chapter 6.

ROMANCE CHECK-IN:
SIXTY WAYS TO SAY "I LOVE YOU"

Today's Date _____ ("calendar" date, which will vary depending how
often you want to check in with your small group or a friend)

Lifetime Date_____ (the "romantic" kind, that is, your spouse)

There are countless ways of romancing your wife, only some of which are listed
here. Think back to when you were dating: How did you go about romancing
your future bride? We assume you put some effort into it. You didn't win her at
a raffle or order her from a Sears catalogue, but you consistently built into her
the assurance of your love. This checklist is for your own information—to
affirm what you are doing currently, to remind yourself of covenant promises
you've already made, and to expand your horizons about what more you could
be doing. In the space beside each item, write a number from 0 to 7 for how
often you have done with your wife each of the sixty ways of loving.

> 0 = Never
> 1 = Once in our relationship
> 2 = Two to five times in our relationship
> 3 = Occasionally, an average of once a year
> 4 = Frequently, but less than once a month
> 5 = Often throughout the month
> 6 = Almost daily, but at least twice weekly
> 7 = Daily, you must still be honeymooners!

For a quick or summary version of this checklist, tabulate the **bold** categories
only. We recommend taking this test periodically, comparing and improving
your progress in the romance department. Each month you'll want to choose
from some such list "something old and something new" to keep romancing
your mate, as God in Christ has romanced you.

____   **1. SAYING "I LOVE YOU" WITH WORDS**
____   2. I expressed appreciation for how my partner works, cooks, cleans,
       dresses, etc.
____   3. I called my partner by a special nickname or term of endearment.
____   4. I whispered "sweet nothings" on her voice mail or phone recorder.
____   5. I dedicated a billboard, lawn sign, banner, graffiti, personals ad, or a
       favorite song on the radio to her.
____   6. I made up a poem instead of a store-bought card.
____   7. I left love notes on sticky pads, on icy windshields, or on steamy bath-
       room mirrors.
____   8. I sent postcards or E-mail to my wife while on a business trip.

____ **9. SAYING "I LOVE YOU" WITH SERVICE**

____ 10. I did errands around town (shopping, etc.), so she could have a special stay-at-home time by herself.

____ 11. I did chores around the house (laundry, meals, the kids' homework and bedtime routines), so she could have some special time *out of* the house.

____ 12. I drove out of my way to chauffeur her somewhere or to bring her home something she requested.

____ 13. I washed and cleaned her car, inside and out.

____ 14. I got her breakfast in bed.

____ 15. I performed a "random act of senseless kindness"—with no thought of a return favor.

____ 16. I treated her as Queen for a day, constantly at her beck and call.

____ **17. SAYING "I LOVE YOU" WITH GIFTS**

____ 18. I was frugal with myself so that I could spoil her with something extra special.

____ 19. I bought her flowers for a special occasion, or for no reason at all.

____ 20. I gave her the gift of affirmation by telling her all the things she does just right and praised her in front of the children.

____ 21. I gave her the gift of merriment by doing something zany, cracking a good joke, wearing a cheerful countenance.

____ 22. I bought her a balloon bouquet, box of her favorite candy, or something else totally frivolous but thoughtful.

____ **23. SAYING "I LOVE YOU" WITH SPECIAL "DATES"**

____ 24. We dressed up to party on New Year's Eve, Valentine's Day, St. Patrick's, July 4th, Halloween, etc.

____ 25. We packed the kids up, took them to grandma's, came back home and spent the weekend alone—just the two of us.

____ 26. We played tourist in the nearest big city and went hotel-hopping, looking for all the night life.

____ 27. We camped out at a nearby campground—or in our back yard.

____ 28. We built a leaf pile, snow sculpture, or sand castle—whatever was in season.

____ 29. We did the old standby—"dinner out and a movie" (or a play).

____ 30. We did the cheaper version of the old standby—dinner *in* and a rented movie or favorite TV show.

____ **31. SAYING "I LOVE YOU" WITH SPORTS DATES**

____ 32. Wild and wacky sports—hot-air ballooning, parasailing, hang gliding, etc.

____ 33. Indoor sports with other couples—dancing lessons, bowling league, volleyball league, bridge club, etc.

___ 34. Indoor sports with just your partner—dancing, aerobics program, racquet sports, etc.
___ 35. Spectator sports—local college teams, Little League teams, etc.
___ 36. Water sports—swimming, snorkeling, scuba diving, water-skiing, sailing, canoeing, fishing, etc.
___ 37. Summer sports—tennis, coed softball team, golf, etc.
___ 38. Winter sports—skating, sledding, cross-country or downhill skiing, etc.

___ **39. Saying "I Love You" by Spending "Time With"**
___ 40. We walked the dog together.
___ 41. We sat on a park bench, sidewalk cafe, or front porch, talking about whatever came up.
___ 42. We held hands (without leading to something else).
___ 43. I fetched the newspaper and we read it together.
___ 44. We walked through the park or zoo or fields, watching people, animals, a sunset, or whatever.
___ 45. We listened to a free open-air concert.
___ 46. We went on a picnic together, following a drive in the country.
___ 47. We went window-shopping or garage saling (without buying a thing).

___ **48. Saying "I Love You" with Affection and Intimacy**
___ 49. We cuddled in front of a fire.
___ 50. We behaved like school kids—"sitting in a tree, k-i-s-s-i-n-g."
___ 51. I made a point of hugging her several times—just for survival, maintenance, and long-term growth of our relationship.
___ 52. I made significant eye contact that turned normal conversation with her into something romantic.

___ **53. Saying "I Love You" by Doing a Joint Mission**
___ 54. We volunteered together at a hospital or nursing home.
___ 55. We took a handicapped or orphaned child on a kid's day out.
___ 56. We served meals on wheels or at a soup kitchen.
___ 57. We entered a walkathon or jogged for a worthy cause.
___ 58. We gave an inner city or overseas mission work project our volunteer labor.
___ 59. We engaged in some other mission together (name it): . . . .

___ **60. We have a totally other way of expressing "I Love You" . . .**

6

WHATEVER HAPPENED TO ROMANCE AND FUN?

HOW DID IT GO?
1. What happened when you discussed the "Romance Check-In" with your wife? Have you made any plans for dates?

THOUGHTS TO PONDER
How do I love thee? Let me count the ways.
I love thee to the depth and breadth and height
My soul can reach, when feeling out of sight
For the ends of Being and ideal Grace.
. . . I love thee with the breath,
Smiles, tears, of all my life:—and if God choose,
I shall love thee better after death.
  —ELIZABETH BARRETT BROWNING (1806–1861)

I belong to my lover,
  and his desire is for me.
Come, my lover, let us go to the countryside,
  let us spend the night in the villages.
Let us go early to the vineyards
  to see if the vines have budded,
if their blossoms have opened,
  and if the pomegranates are in bloom—
  there I will give you my love.
  —THE BELOVED (SONG OF SONGS 7:10-12)

The lack of dating and romance is one of the major causes of a broken relationship. Marriages usually don't collapse overnight. They become

79

bankrupt gradually because they lack daily deposits of love, communication, and affirmation. . . . If you want to add life to your marriage, perhaps even save its life, you'd better do whatever it takes to bring romance and dating back into the picture.
—DOUG FIELDS

Men and women view the beginning, middle, and end stages of romance differently. In stating that as my premise, I do not want to stereotype anyone. But the stories I share here tend to corroborate differences in the way men and women typically view romance and fun in marriage.

Romance Is No Big Deal, but Consistency in the Little Things Is What Counts

Quite often men equate romance with sex in their marital relationship. However, women generally equate romance with a relationship that is growing, maturing, and making her feel special, whether or not it leads to sex.

Men also tend to place romance within a series of big events or extravagant happenings. That's how we score in the business world, so we think we can score husbanding points with big creative dates. Don't knock it 'til you've tried it, which I did on a recent road trip.

Since speaking and training events for men take me so far afield these days, I have not had the time with my wife and family we desire. Hence, I arranged to have Susan join me on a recent trip to California. She knew none of the details, except "we would have time together." When we arrived at the airport, I used coupons from mileage programs to bump us to first class, a mode of travel she had never before experienced (now she'll be spoiled). Upon arriving in California, the car rental agency gave us the upgrade I had secretly requested (and redeemed coupons for): a red convertible. My wife has always wanted to own and drive a red convertible. We spent one day simply driving the coastal highway, talking, looking, stopping at points of interest, taking in a quiet lunch—a memory-making enjoyable time together. I sure scored some husbanding points that day.

Although such memory-making, point-scoring dates are appreciated by every woman with a pulse, most women want you to take their pulse—that is, ask them what their pleasure is and then do it. For the women I've counseled or interviewed, and for the one I married, consistency and kindness by men is what's most romantic.

Romance is not some test we suddenly cram for. Romance is a day-in and day-out proposition, seizing the moment to show love and affection. It's asking what soft drink your wife wants when you raid the refrigerator for yourself. Or fetching the morning paper for her to read in bed. Mrs. Browning's classic love poems, *Sonnets from the Portuguese*, penned while an invalid during her reluctant marriage to Robert, amply testify to the healing power of his romantic love lived out day to day in rather mundane service and cramped circumstances.

As I have met and counseled with married men over the years, I am intrigued by how many don't know how to romance their wives in the little ways that mean so much. When I ask these men what they did when they were dating, they are full of good ideas (as reflected in the "Romance Check-In"). Sometime after the wedding ceremony and honeymoon, selective amnesia and smug indifference take over, as men simply neglect to romance their wives and keep a good thing going.

Consider, for example, the stoic, strong-and-silent guy in marriage counseling with his wife of many years. She tells the counselor, "But he never tells me that he loves me." To which the husband retorts, "I told you I loved you when we got married. If anything changes, I'll let you know."

Come on, guys. Whatever happened to romance and fun in your marriage? Gone are the days when you used to open the door for her to get into the car. No longer do you encourage her to sit next to you when you drive. You used to buy her flowers and candy; now you can't even remember to send her a card. Gone are the weekly nights out and occasional "creative dates"—humdrum routine took their place.

Our wives want to be romanced—as if you didn't know! If you are not sure how to romance your wife effectively, simply ask her. You will be surprised to find out that romancing her need not be expensive; rather, consistency is what counts. For instance, I used to buy roses for my wife on various occasions. I thought I was scoring big points, yet there was always minimal response. When I finally asked why, I learned that Susan saw cut flowers as wasteful. (She prefers living plants, although we joke about the fact that their life expectancy in our house is not much longer than a cut flower's.) I also learned along the way it was more romantic to bring her a half-gallon of chocolate ice cream than to get her a card. So, men, unless you can read minds better than I can—ask.

Experiment with the various fun items on the "Romance Check-In." Ask questions. Learn together. Don't focus on just the candlelit dinners at home or a meal out at her favorite restaurant. Remember the little things—helping out, offering praise, a tender look—build romance.

Some Guys Have All the Romantic Flair of a Dish Rag

I remember counseling with one man (I'll call him "Ed") who was completely exasperated that his wife didn't feel loved and was threatening to leave. Ed assured me he was doing all the right "things." Yet he couldn't understand why she was feeling so rejected. When I asked him, "What things?" he listed all he could think of: working hard, bringing home a paycheck, providing her with a house, and thanking her for a well-cooked dinner.

While trying hard to maintain a straight face, I pointed out to this poor man his utter lack of romantic flair. No wonder she felt unloved—Ed showed her no love. To generate some new ideas, I had him list what they did when they were dating. (You, too, will have a chance to take a trip down memory lane and recall some of your most memorable dates.) I had Ed speak to several older men in the church about what they were doing to keep romance alive in their marriages. For the man who has difficulty understanding how to compliment his wife or use romantic language, I often give him the Song of Songs as a reading assignment. As the list of ideas grew for Ed, so did his excitement level. He couldn't wait to try out what he had rediscovered about loving his wife.

Men Usually Love the Chase More Than the Catch

On July 29, 1981, some 750 million people, one out of every six people in the world, watched the "wedding of the century" that took place in England. About that wedding between Prince Charles and Lady Diana, the Archbishop of Canterbury made this telling statement:

> Here is the stuff of which fairy tales are made—the Prince and the Princess on their wedding day. But fairy tales usually

end at this point with the simple phrase, "They lived happily ever after." This may be because fairy tales regard marriage as an anti-climax after romance and courtship and the wedding. This is not the Christian view.

How true. Men usually love the chase more than the catch, so we back off the romance after our last big date—the wedding. Yet dating your mate should not stop then. Before you married her, you did everything possible to assure your romantic interest that you loved her. Why not continue on that course? Wouldn't it be incredible if we husbands spent as much time, if not more, seeking to please our mates *after* the marriage vows are spoken as beforehand? Before the marriage, we kept on saying, "Can I help you?" But after we're hitched, it's more often, "Help me." It is time to turn the clock back, men.

The unmarried Apostle Paul was a realist about this very point. "An unmarried man is concerned about the Lord's affairs—how he can please the Lord. But a married man is concerned about the affairs of this world—how he can please his wife" (1 Corinthians 7:32-33). That may sound like an indictment of marriage, that a husband can't really serve his Lord effectively because he is preoccupied with pleasing his wife. Yet Paul is saying something positive here about the reality and validity of the wife's needs. A married man is concerned with pleasing his wife—that's as it should be!

In romancing my wife, the key issue is, am I seeking to please her?

Some Guys *Do* Understand the Power of Romancing Their Wives

On a recent flight, I was reading a book on marriage, trying to glean a few ideas for writing this book. It was the third leg of a trip, and I was tired and stiff, so I walked to the back of the plane, stood near the galley, and resumed my reading there. The plane wasn't all that full, and the flight attendant was mostly finished with her tasks, so out of politeness she asked me what I was reading. I showed her, which made her more curious. She asked me what I did, so I explained the speaking and training seminars I do with men.

Then I involved her in my writing project. "Perhaps you can

help me out. I'm working on a chapter in a study guide for a men's small group, a chapter on how to build romance in your marriage. Let me ask you, what things does your husband do that build romance or show care and concern in your marriage?"

She started bragging about her husband, an English literature professor at a midwestern university, but then caught me off guard with this comment: "Well, you know, the more I think about it, it's not really the big things. It's the little things. Don't get me wrong. I like receiving jewelry and other nice gifts. But it's the little things that my husband has chosen to do that enhance my feeling of acceptance, affirmation, and love."

I asked her to elaborate and she did. Every morning, even if they are away on a trip, her husband always brings her a morning cup of coffee in bed, even at times when he's had to drive to a convenience store to get one. She said, "That makes me feel loved." A second thing he does is this: No matter who travels where, or where she is spending the night, home or away—every night he calls her. Thirdly, he will intentionally find "excuses" so he *can* drive her to work. He always makes sure the radio is off so they can simply talk in the car. She went on and on, waxing eloquent about the little things he did, as if extending Mrs. Browning's poem, "Let me count the ways." Now there's a man who understands the power of romancing his wife!

Romance Is Having Fun with Your Mate, with No Other Agenda

To profit from what I have to say about fun and laughter, you should understand that I am a very focused, intense, and introverted person. Perhaps that's why I like to laugh—it focuses one's attention and dispels all thoughts of depression or stress or other agendas. You should also know that, despite my healthy sense of humor, I am not exactly the life-of-the-party type.

For instance, when my children were little and given tricycles with noisy clackers attached to the spokes, I removed them. I told my kids, "You now have a new, highly sophisticated silent machine that can swoop in, undetected, through enemy radar." They bought it! I am also the one who, when my son was little and given a tom-tom to play with, asked him, "Have you ever seen what's inside one of these things?" You know what happened.

Though I like quiet and solitude (no clackers or tom-toms), I have learned tremendous lessons about other kinds of fun. As enjoyable as sight-seeing may be for adults, it is not exactly on the "Top Ten" list for my children. I have also learned that when visiting some historic site, never ever call it a vacation. An "educational field trip" will do, or "expanding one's horizon," but not the word *vacation,* which for my children, at least, means "fun." They want to visit weird places, lie on the beach, or swim until they turn blue from cold, spring water. They'll spend extended time laughing with Mom and Dad, but hate hours on end driving somewhere to see where some historical figure is buried.

We men often think there must be an agenda anytime we get together. If someone calls up and asks, "Let's do lunch," we typically respond, "What's up?" We approach lunch dates with our wives with the same agenda-consciousness. During fun times with your wife, let her know you are with her just to be with her—no other agenda.

Your Only Agenda Is to Experience Fun and Enjoy Each Other

This was dramatically brought home to me by our friends who provide alternate sleep-over arrangements and fun ideas for our children. Almost always our children come home from Aunt Karen and Uncle Duck's with some new, crazy idea. Once they came home with ideas for a "Noise Night." That's when all family members and guests are given a pot or pan and a utensil to bang with. For a predetermined length of time, players make all the noise they want—banging, yelling, laughing, and carrying on.

Another time this crazy family donned plastic trash bags with holes cut out for the heads and arms; then, armed with cans of shaving cream, they were turned loose to "cream" one another. Another night, this time during our Bible study there, a food fight broke out between all the couples and their kids, a fun fiasco which didn't end until we had to sit down to keep from laughing so hard.

Romancing Your Wife Means Enjoying Her Personal Idiosyncrasies

We dwell on little quirks in our spouse or in our families so often that we have forgotten how to laugh about differences and the foolish things that happen. In other words, putting the romance and fun back in your marriage is not only about creative fun and games. Having a sense of humor in the midst of crises and chaos is half the fun of being a family. When yielded to the Spirit of God, we are free to laugh when life tries to make us feel upset or drift apart.

Case in point: My wife mistakenly put my trousers into the wash without checking the back pocket (which I realize is my task, not hers). This time, my wallet, credit cards, and money came out dripping wet and smelling Downy soft. With Susan wondering how to dry out my wallet and me running out on a brief errand, I simply yelled back, "Whatever you do, don't put it in the microwave."

When I arrived home, thirty minutes later, our dinner guests had arrived and were staring at this strange, lumpy, brown mound sitting on the countertop by the microwave. Immediately, I knew what had happened and began laughing. This got my wife laughing, but left our guest audience even more bewildered. So I said, impishly, "Looks like yesterday's meat loaf, doesn't it?" Then everyone joined in our laughter.

Moral of the story for men who would be romantic: Why get angry over mishaps or plan big romantic deals to make up for lost time, when you can draw close through enjoying humor in the crazy things and crisis events that happen in your everyday life together?

Lighten Up; He Who Laughs—Lasts

On another occasion, when visiting with friends at Christmas time, the host husband had fastened little white Christmas lights to their floor-to-ceiling stone fireplace. Susan asked how they were put up, and he replied, "With a hot glue gun." That got her wheels turning. A few days later, when I noticed a similar, but very straight, display of Christmas lights on the outside windows of our house, I asked Susan how they had been installed. She informed me, with a smile of accomplishment, "With a hot glue gun." For a number of years, the hot glue gun has been Susan's fix-it-all remedy for just about everything in the house.

The big difference between gluing lights to the outside window of our house and gluing lights to our friends' fireplace is this. The surface around our windows was all wood; not only did the glue peel the paint off when we tried to remove the lights, but

Susan had glued every single bulb in place to guarantee they were straight. Years later, when we sold our house and moved across town, those Christmas lights were still there. As always, laughter was the best medicine.

Laughter can't change the light bulbs, but it can get us to lighten up. Which reminds all of us: Have a little fun, laugh a little bit, and enjoy the lighter side of life together. Irritants become opportunities to grow together when we laugh at them. He who laughs—lasts.

WHAT DO YOU THINK?

2. With which of the stories of men who would be romantics could you most identify with and why?

☐ Glenn's memory-making, point-scoring date in California.

☐ The mundane service of a Robert Browning to his invalid wife, Elizabeth, whose famous love poem is a tribute to undying devotion.

☐ The men of selective amnesia and smug indifference, who forget how they ever romanced their spouses in the first place.

☐ The stiff, strong-and-silent type who said, "I told you I loved you when we got married. If anything changes, I'll let you know."

☐ Ed, exasperated because his wife didn't feel loved, but teachable; he did assigned homework and learned to romance her.

☐ Prince Charles and Lady Diana, for whom courtship was everything romantic, and marriage was anything but "happily ever after."

☐ Men who once went out of their way to serve ("Can I help you?"), but since the wedding have become more demanding ("Help me!").

☐ The flight attendant's husband, a man who knew the power of romancing his wife in little things (coffee, car rides, phone calls).

☐ Uncle Duck, someone full of creative games and fun dates.

3. Put yourself in the all-too-familiar scenario of the husband-and-wife couple who are your friends, but have lost the romantic spark in their marriage. The husband comes to you seeking counsel about what to do to bring romance back and save his loveless marriage. He is eager to do whatever it takes to score husbanding points. What would you say to him?

4. If it's true that God in Christ "romanced us to Himself" through the Cross and poured His compelling grace into our hearts (2 Corinthians 5:18-19), then you are a new creation, a lover of God, an ambassador for Christ. What is more, you are renewed in your commitment to actively romance your wife. The Song of Songs can help you in that regard. Many interpret this song between two lovers as analogous to Christ romancing His bride, the Church.

Assign one of the seven "stanzas" in this classic love poem to each man in the group. (Scripture divisions and titles are excerpted below from the *Serendipity Bible for Groups.*[1]) Each man should read his assigned stanza and try to discern: (1) how God might be loving you in the way(s) described in the sonnet; and, by extension, (2) how your love might become "aroused" and "sweeter than wine" for your beloved. Allow five minutes for reading, thinking, and jotting notes, then discuss what you've observed.

■ Song of Songs 1:1–2:7 / The First Meeting: "The Bud of Romance"
■ Song of Songs 2:8–3:5 / The Second Meeting: "The Blossom of Courtship"
■ Song of Songs 3:6-11 / The Third Meeting: "The Wedding Song"
■ Song of Songs 4:1–5:1 / The Fourth Meeting: "Some Enchanted Evening"
■ Song of Songs 5:2–6:3 / The Fifth Meeting: "The Absence of the Lover"
■ Song of Songs 6:4–7:9a / The Sixth Meeting: "The Return of Love"
■ Song of Songs 7:9b–8:14 / The Climactic Meeting: "A Romp in the Woods"

TRY IT AT HOME
5. "Show and Tell"

They say a picture is worth a thousand words, so at the beginning of your next session, cut down on your talk time and let four snapshots from your family photo album do the talking for you. Bring to that session four representative photos:

a. your early dating life with your wife
b. your courtship days
c. your wedding or honeymoon
d. your current dating life

If (a) or (b) is a blur, or if no camera was present (at the school sock hop, office party, ski outing, campus seminar, or whatever), then you can double up on pictures from (c) and (d). For pictures or poses that group members have questions about, please recite a brief caption.

6. (Optional) Try some of the lines from the Song of Songs on your wife this week. If you're new to the romantic poetry game, just try reading some of it to her. If you're an advanced player, improvise.

7. "Win with Me"

Try asking your wife at least one of the following questions:

■ Honey, what's weighing particularly heavily on you right now?
■ Sweetheart, is there any way that I can help share your load and keep you from knuckling under that weight?
■ Honey, I've been dealing with my own heavy stuff and have neglected your needs. Now I want a win-win solution that will make life easier or better for both of us. How can I help you win with me?

Report your wife's answer to a trusted member of your group before the next meeting.

8. Set aside time to play the "Remember When . . . ?" game (pages 91-92) with your wife. Your notes can be as brief as you want, prompted by sneak peeks at your family album (see question 5). Other memory-joggers are supplied on the worksheet. This exercise should be a lot of fun for you as a couple and may be the basis for a future get-together in which all group members and their wives gather to share their stories.

9. As you read chapter 7 in preparation for the next session, begin thinking of ways you could be making time with your partner. Sometimes we overcommit ourselves to activities outside the home, robbing us of the time and energy to be a true companion to our beloved. You will learn more about making companionship time and keeping those promises in the next chapter.

    Be sure to bring your appointment book or calendar to the next group meeting.

NOTE
1. *Serendipity Bible for Groups,* edited by Lyman Coleman and Dietrich Gruen (Littleton, CO: Serendipity House, 1989), page 865.

"REMEMBER WHEN . . . ?"
A Trip Down Memory Lane

For a Christmas gift one year, a third grader named Mark made a "Remember When" book for his father. He had especially prepared the book with pencil and crayon drawings, all neatly captioned with questions that began, "Remember when . . . ?" ("Remember when I learned to ride my bike without training wheels?" "Remember when we were in Massachusetts visiting Gram when Hurricane Bob struck?")

The pictures and captions did help the father remember, but what pleased this dad even more was that these great father-son times were also memory-makers for the son. Preserved in that book, they helped rekindle the desire of the whole family for memorable events that draw everyone together.

This exercise is like that book. It's a multi-year reflection for men and their wives to "remember when." Here are a few triggers to jog your memory:

- Your first date and/or your first kiss.
- First impressions and nicknames you have for each other.
- The first gifts you exchanged.
- When you popped "the question," and she said. . . .
- Places you visited on the first honeymoon or a recent getaway.
- Crises you resolved after your honeymoon.
- Something funny that happened to you while you were. . . .

Didn't that brief memory-jogger bring and keep a smile on your face? Having started your trip down memory lane, ask yourself what you saw in each other along the way. Jot down in the space below your trip notes for at least six memorable moments that drew you and your wife closer together during three major periods of your life together.

If you have photos, attach them. If you have an artistic bent, draw pictures. With or without pictures, write out captions that will serve as memory-joggers of the things you used to do when dating, courting, or romancing your wife.

Be sure to focus on the whole span of time that you have known her, including the last six to twelve months, not just your courtship or honeymoon days. If a vivid picture comes to mind—great—just write down the word for it under the event, then the date (don't worry if you can't remember the exact date, the nearest year is close enough) and then the caption that goes with it.

In your men's group, hold yourself accountable for at least having jotted some notes in the spaces below. If you have time during a fellowship hour to tell the story behind the event and caption, your time will be rewarded. The point of this exercise is to make your trip list now, on your own, then later to have your wife do the same. Afterwards, schedule a date night to compare notes, enjoy old photos and a joint trip down memory lane.

A. Memory Makers of the Months/Years That I Was Courting My Mate

	Event	Date	Caption
A.1.			
A.2.			
A.3.			
A.4.			
A.5.			
A.6.			

B. Memory Makers Spanning All the Years of Our Life Together

(Picture one for every year, or one for every two or three years if yours is a long marriage.)

	Event	Date	Caption
B.1.			
B.2.			
B.3.			
B.4.			
B.5.			
B.6.			

C. Memory Makers of the Last 6-12 Months of Our Life Together

	Event	Date	Caption
C.1.			
C.2.			
C.3.			
C.4.			
C.5.			
C.6.			

Identify the three most meaningful memory-makers, one from each list above. Circle the number corresponding to that event. As you think about these three, ask yourself: Why is this a meaningful moment? How did it make me feel about myself? About my wife? Jot down a few notes for sharing with your spouse.

Pick one story to share in your study group as time permits, or after hours one-on-one if group time does not permit. This is no time for one-upmanship, but a time to stimulate one another to love and good works.

7

MAKING TIME WITH YOUR WIFE

HOW DID IT GO?
1. Did you do the "Remember When...?" exercise? What did you discover?

We've saved "Show and Tell" and "Win with Me" (questions 5 and 7 of chapter 6) for the end of this session because they have the potential to devour all of your time.

THOUGHTS TO PONDER
¹There is a time for everything,
and a season for every activity under heaven:
²a time to be born and a time to die,
a time to plant and a time to uproot,
³a time to kill and a time to heal,
a time to tear down and a time to build,
⁴a time to weep and a time to laugh,
a time to mourn and a time to dance,
⁵a time to scatter stones and a time to gather them,
a time to embrace and a time to refrain,
⁶a time to search and a time to give up,
a time to keep and a time to throw away,
⁷a time to tear and a time to mend,
a time to be silent and a time to speak,
⁸a time to love and a time to hate,
a time for war and a time for peace.
⁹What does the worker gain from his toil? ¹⁰I have seen the bur-
den God has laid on men. ¹¹He has made everything beautiful in its

time. He has also set eternity in the hearts of men; yet they cannot fathom what God has done from beginning to end. [12]I know that there is nothing better for men than to be happy and do good while they live. [13]That everyone may eat and drink, and find satisfaction in all his toil—this is the gift of God. [14]I know that everything God does will endure forever; nothing can be added to it and nothing taken from it. God does it so that men will revere him.
[15]Whatever is has already been,
and what will be has been before;
and God will call the past to account.
    —THE TEACHER (ECCLESIASTES 3:1-15)

Time is . . .
Too slow for those who wait,
Too swift for those who fear,
Too long for those who grieve,
Too short for those who rejoice,
But for those who love,
Time is eternity.
    —HENRY VAN DYKE

For years I have listened to the debate concerning "quality time" versus "quantity of time." As young seminarians and pastors, we tried to map out the perfect schedule. That whole debate begs questions such as, "Are you just marking time, killing time, and/or 'doing' time?" Criminals do that much. On the other hand, are you spending time, investing time, or "making" time? That's what counts for eternity.

Time is a gift from God entrusted to my care that I am to spend or invest wisely. As this gift of time, and the debate surrounding it, applies to my spouse, the question becomes, "How am I investing my time in my wife?" (Am I remembering birthdays, special occasions and events? Am I available for special needs, crises, and problems as they arise? Am I investing time in fun activities?)

Love Is Spelled T-I-M-E

When I was newly married, a wise senior pastor once told me the best way to spell *love* is "T-I-M-E." He never told me how much was enough, nor how little would destroy my marriage. The gas gauge tells you when your car is running on empty, but no comparable time gauge tells you when your marriage is running on empty. We might lull ourselves into thinking we have enough time for renewing relationships with the people we love, but we would never dare be so neglectful or indifferent about refueling the cars we drive.

As you gauge how much time you invest in the priorities that matter most, rest assured that an inordinate amount of time spent on the job does not necessarily make you a workaholic or a materialist. I realize that for many men, a long-hour, high-stress job is simply the nature of their business; they have no other choice if they want to support their family. Everyone compromises or compensates on the home front in pursuit of a win-win solution to the time crunch.

Years ago, an older friend of mine who traveled extensively was staying at our house while speaking at our church. He talked with Susan and me about his wife's frustration and discouragement with his travel schedule. That started Susan reflecting on the whole issue of "how much hubby is home." She had never spoken to me directly about this issue before. Susan recounted a period in our marriage when she was completely frustrated with the amount of time I was away from the house. In anger (and Susan is not given to anger), she kicked the door and had a good cry. Without realizing it, she had become bitter at my work, which she felt was driving a wedge in our relationship. Yet she wanted to free me to pursue what God had called me—and us—to do.

What struck me was this insight: Susan knew I *wanted* to be home and be with her, even when I couldn't be. Reassurance of that desire on my part made the difference in her attitude, sense of security, and well-being. She could endure the times I had to be away, without harmful thoughts or painful memories. My responsibility then was not only to make time to be with her, but to let her know there was nothing I would rather do than be with her. That means when I went with her to the mall (not my idea of fun), I did not sulk or whine. Although I may feel humiliation when left standing in the midst of the women's lingerie department (I often think she intentionally sneaks off, simply to watch me turn red with embarrassment), I let her know that time with her is more important than the places we go (or where I'm left standing).

Yet, as an old sage once pointed out, we can make time for what we want—embracing, loving, building up, laughing, mourning—because God subjects "every activity under heaven," even the "hearts of men," to His eternal and sovereign purposes (Ecclesiastes 3:1-15). Under the sovereign hand of God, we schedule our time to make sure we do the "important," not necessarily the "urgent."

Make Time for Significant Events

The most significant activity I do is not serving as the Vice President of Promise Keepers. It is not speaking at conferences and training seminars, nor is it meeting publisher's deadlines for writing projects. The most important role I fulfill in life is being a godly husband for my wife, Susan, and a loving dad for my children, Haven and Justin. I seek to structure my time in such a way that I am present for their significant events and special occasions.

Make Time for Special Needs in Their Lives

I can't schedule my ministry and travels around the crises and problems that arise. "Life happens" without advance notice, usually while you're doing something else. I never know when my wife will have a difficult or stressful day, so I make myself available anyway, even if only by a long distance phone call. Susan also knows she can interrupt my work whenever a special need arises.

Make Time for One-on-One *Serendipities*

I keep a tight schedule, as many men do. I know better than to wait for one-on-one times to simply "happen." They don't. Appointments that get on my schedule invariably crowd out unscheduled happenings. Hence, regular one-on-one times need to be scheduled, worked on, and developed with high priority.

Sometimes one-on-one time is nothing more than a walk. Other times it means putting the kids to bed early for our own cuddle time by the fireside. Other one-on-ones involve a trip to the mall or grocery store when one person could just as easily have gone alone. The seclusion of the car also allows for one-on-one trips into the country, to out-of-the-way dinner spots, or a breakfast date to start the day right.

Not only do I schedule one-on-one times for just the two of us, I enjoy impromptu, serendipitous times together with my wife. Such *serendipities*, or "happy chance discoveries," are a fun part of life with Susan. Occasionally I miss out, and I'm the poorer for it. I need to make time—in my heart as well as on the calendar—so that when serendipities come our way, I can seize the fun opportunity.

Make Time for Companionship to Develop Within Your Marriage

Companionship time involves much more than simply being in the same place at the same time. When traveling cross-country alone, I can still sense a tremendous companionship with Susan. I love being with her; times apart from her do not diminish our companionship, but may actually enhance it. We need spaces in our togetherness.

As Martin Luther said, "Let the wife make her husband glad to come home and let him make her sorry to see him leave." Dietrich and Suzanne have a different twist on Luther's benediction than Susan and I do. He works at home, sometimes burying himself in his basement office; also, his wife travels more in her job than my wife does. Because our wives each know that we would rather be with them than with anyone else or any place else, a keen sense of companionship bridges the miles and the mealtimes spent apart.

Over the years, when doing the funerals for church members and spending time with the surviving spouse, I have sensed that kind of companionship. One dear widow told me that every evening they used to go to the window, gaze at the moon or the sky, and thank God for each other, for the beauty of that shared day and the joy of one another's company. What she missed most about him was that sense of companionship, which had flourished for over forty years of marriage.

Susan loves to watch football. Believe it or not, when the NFL Game of the Week is on TV, she controls the programming at our house. No matter how strong the preferences of another child or adult, the TV football game belongs to Mom. (Her territoriality could have something to do with having grown up with six brothers.) That's the way it is at the Wagners on Sunday afternoons or Monday nights in the fall—a total reversal of what most men experience, I realize. Since I "like" football but don't "love" it, I've learned one way I can love Susan is by spending part of that time with her, instead of going off by myself to read or study.

Companionship time tells Susan I love her like nothing else does. There is no substitute for companionship—just ask your wife.

WHAT DO YOU THINK?

2. What is your reaction to the never-ending debate entitled, "How much is hubby home?"

☐ I don't have time for such discussions; I skipped this section.
☐ When I relax at home, I feel guilty that I should be at work.
☐ When I am busy at work, I feel guilty that I should be at home.
☐ I'm one of those who marks time, kills time, or does time.
☐ I may manage time well enough, but I'm not very spontaneous.
☐ I would feel awkward "scheduling" my partner.

3. Which of the following characterizes how you spend time (fill in the blank):

☐ For me, time is too slow, especially when I wait for . . . .
☐ For me, time is too swift, especially when I fear . . . .
☐ For me, time is too long, especially when I grieve . . . .
☐ For me, time is too short, especially when I rejoice in . . . .
☐ For me, time is eternal, especially when I love . . . .

4. Put yourself in the ironic scenario of Glenn, the husband who is obliged to spend Sunday afternoons or Monday nights watching NFL football if he wants to spend time with his wife.

a. What must that be like for the husband who values companionship time with his wife, but doesn't really like to watch football?

b. By the way, who controls the television in your household on the weekends? How do you convert passive TV watching into something more interactive?

c. Glenn will also go to malls and stand in long lines to be with his wife. To what extent will you go to be with your wife?

d. Glenn was somehow able to assure his wife that his *desire* to be with her, even though he had to be apart, was one way to win the "how much is hubby home" dilemma. How do you win that one in your household?

5. Glenn challenges us with the closing statement, "There is no substitute for companionship—just ask your wife."

a. Do you agree with him? (Could it be that happier couples just decide to spend more time together, or does spending time together lead to more successful marriages?)

b. What might your wife say about this if you ask her later this week?

6. Last session you were assigned homework to find out what needs or concerns your wife had that you might carry or help her to "win with you." You were to report your findings to a trusted member of your men's group. Did you do that? Is there anything from your findings that you can share with the rest of the group for prayer? Take as much time as you want to meet the needs of your respective wives through praying for them.

7. In affirming that people have little control over what happens to them, and that all times and changing circumstances are subject to God's eternal and sovereign purposes (Ecclesiastes 3:1-15), would you say that the biblical author

is a realist, a pessimist, a skeptic, or a believer? Explain your answer.

8. Of the fourteen opposites listed in Ecclesiastes 3:2-8, which times have you or your spouse experienced in a significant way? (For example, births or miscarriages would fit verse 2; divorce could fit many "times.") Tell the group about one or more of these times they don't necessarily know about.

- a time to be born
- a time to plant
- a time to kill
- a time to tear down
- a time to weep
- a time to mourn
- a time to scatter stones
- a time to embrace
- a time to search
- a time to keep
- a time to tear
- a time to be silent
- a time to love
- a time for war

- a time to die
- a time to uproot
- a time to heal
- a time to build
- a time to laugh
- a time to dance
- a time to gather them
- a time to refrain
- a time to give up
- a time to throw away
- a time to mend
- a time to speak
- a time to hate
- a time for peace

9. If you wanted to spend more one-on-one time with your wife, and we hope you do, what changes in your schedule would you, or could you, make now? Which of the following how-to suggestions might work for you?

☐ Shift who performs household chores and/or child care.
☐ Demand more flex time in our respective jobs outside the home.
☐ Set a weekly date night—and no exceptions to the "sacred time."
☐ Look upward and inward and take more time for self-renewal, so that I am not so needy or demanding of my spouse.

☐ Take on the hobbies or interests of the other, drop one of my own, or find a new one in common.

☐ Adjust the body clock of each mate so that we match as either "morning larks" or "night owls."

☐ Wait for the kids to grow up and move out, then I'll have time to get reacquainted with my wife.

☐ Do the "mundane" things together and thereby make them "special."

☐ Take turns regarding whose "day" it is: that person determines what we do together; we agree in advance that the other mate cannot say no.

☐ Write (with my partner) our own "sixty ways" for doing the "Romance Check-In"; then do one a day for the next sixty days.

☐ Start small—settle for a few ten-minute activities together per week; build up to more leisure time together as if we're in a fitness program.

☐ Begin by praying with my wife; prayer has a way of changing us and our schedules (more about this in chapter 8).

10. "Show and Tell" from question 5 of chapter 6.
Last session we asked you to bring in four representative snapshots from your family photo album that would portray you and your beloved at various stages in your dating relationship: (1) your early dating life with your mate; (2) your courtship days; (3) your wedding or honeymoon; (4) your current dating life. We hope you will have something to "show and tell" this week.

TRY IT AT HOME

11. Time management seminars are "a dime a dozen." (Actually, they cost hundreds of dollars more than that.) We offered you a few how-to suggestions here, but we threw in some motivational stories on companionship time with your wife (see the epilogue for two more). The rest is up to you. Make a point of checking in with one another this week, calendars in hand, to encourage success in making time for one-on-ones with your wives.

12. This session you prayed for one another's marriages, especially the burdens your respective wives may be carrying. As you read chapter 8 in preparation for the next session, bring your "Family Mission Statements," which we hope you have completed by now. (You have been working on it ever since session 2, haven't you?) In either event, completed or not, those mission statements will serve as a basis for extended prayer for one another in the men's group. You will learn more about praying with and for your wife in the next chapter.

8

Praying With And For Your Wife

THOUGHTS TO PONDER
Successful marriage is always a triangle: a man, a woman, and God.
—Cecil Myers

[9]For this reason, since the day we heard about you, we have not stopped praying for you and asking God to fill you with the knowledge of his will through all spiritual wisdom and understanding. [10]And we pray this in order that you may live a life worthy of the Lord and may please him in every way: bearing fruit in every good work, growing in the knowledge of God, [11]being strengthened with all power according to his glorious might so that you may have great endurance and patience, and joyfully [12]giving thanks to the Father, who has qualified you to share in the inheritance of the saints in the kingdom of light.
—The Apostle Paul (Colossians 1:9-12)

A key element in strengthening your marriage is prayer. Paul says that "he has not stopped praying" for the Christians at Colosse. By his example we see the importance of praying daily for the people you love. The content and focus of Paul's prayer suggests a number of concerns about which we can be praying for our mates and our family responsibilities.

Pray Your Beloved Will Know the Will of God for Her Life (Verse 9)
Paul prays first that the people he loves will be filled with the knowledge of God's will. Paul says, in effect, "I want you to know, and not only know but experience, the will of God." Is there anything more important than that, as you pray for your

wife and family? That means praying for their salvation, since at this point you may not know whether everyone in your family knows Christ as Savior. Or, if everyone in your family is already a Christian, this will mean praying for their sanctification, that they will grow in the things of God.

Pray for the Lifestyle of Your Beloved (Verse 10)

Paul prays that their "walk"—that is, their moral values and choices—will indeed reflect what God is doing. I cannot think of anything more important to pray for your wife and children. Pray that they will be protected from the evil one, especially during those days when your family members are beyond your grasp, under someone's else care and influence, or beyond any human ability to help.

Pray Against Stagnation; Pray for Her Productivity (Verse 10)

We easily become stagnant in our walk with Jesus Christ. Pray for your wife, that she will have a vibrancy and will not fall into a mere status-quo relationship with God. Pray that your wife's character will not only please the Lord, but that she will also bear fruit and good works for His glory and honor. Pray that she is spiritually growing and productive for the Lord. Uphold her in prayer, that she might have a strong ministry in the lives of others.

Pray for Ability to Overcome Difficult Situations (Verse 11)

We live in a socially complex and morally difficult society, even a kingdom of darkness, which bombards our families with mixed signals and impedes our walk with God. So we need to pray that our wives and children will not be overcome by daily temptation but will be strengthened for spiritual battles in crisis situations. Coach Bill McCartney, founder of the Promise Keepers, declared at PK '93, "Men, you have been in a war, but you have not been *at* war. . . . We contest anything that sets itself up against Jesus Christ." Christian marriages are under attack as never before, and we must wage war against sin and the spiritual forces of evil.

Pray for Her to Have a Joyful, Thankful Attitude (Verses 11-12)

Pray that your wife will rejoice in the things that God has given her to do, that she will see the positive side of God's grace and be thankful for His merciful intervention in your lives, even when that mercy is severe.

Pray for Her to Have a Healthy Self-Concept (Verse 12)

God has qualified us to share in the inheritance of the saints, bringing us into His light. Prayer helps us to fully realize this benefit of having a right relationship with God. Paul prays, in effect, "May you have a right perspective of who you are, to understand that through faith in Jesus Christ you are an inheritor of all the promises and blessings of God. You are someone special." Pray that your wife will understand how special she is in God's sight, and that she will not listen to agents of the evil one seeking to belittle her.

Praying *for* My Wife Is One Thing; Praying *with* Her Is Another

If the history of our nation belongs to the intercessors, and I believe it does, then I believe the history of our marriages also belongs to those who intercede. Knowing and believing this does not always make it happen, however, as many couples find difficulty in meeting together for prayer. They know to pray *for* one another; they just have problems praying *with* one another. Ever find yourself in that boat?

When Susan and I first started dating in college, she already had several years of Bible college and training behind her. (No, she's not older than I am—I was simply a late bloomer.) I remember how intimidated I felt when praying or worshiping with her. When it became obvious this was a potential problem area, she was able to affirm Christian growth in me. She also assured me, and I want to assure you as well, that prayer partnerships are not gauged on who knows more, but only on the desire to grow together in Christ.

Now the tables have turned, and I have the theological degree and the pastoral language down pat. Hence, I am in danger of assuming the role of the teacher, rather than standing on common ground with Susan, as joint heirs of grace (1 Peter 3:7) and fellow students struggling together. But I have to avoid that at all costs. What each marriage needs is a priest, not a preacher—a priest who will seek to minister to the needs of his wife and family.

Coach Mac of Promise Keepers reminds us and models for us what this is all about:

> Almighty God is calling men to pray over their families in such a way that, if a man will pray daily, regularly over his wife, praying for God's blessings upon her, Almighty God will restore her self-image. . . . Our women need a man providing the spiritual tempo and leadership in the home.

When Coach Mac prays for and with his wife, Lyndi, he kneels beside her, lays his arm around her, puts his hand upon her. He then prays something like this (from the prayer he modeled at the 1993 Promise Keepers Conference), which we excerpt here as a model and encouragement for you and your beloved:

> Lord Jesus Christ, I invoke Your power and Your Spirit upon Lyndi. Lord, I pray righteousness and purity and holiness upon her. Lord, I pray that You will heal all of her scars, that You will mend up all those things that keep her from being the woman that she desires to be and that You call her to be.
> Lord God, I pray that You will breathe excitement into her, that You will bring about in Lindy a hope for the future. I pray that I will have favor with her. I pray, Lord, that she will see me and that her heart will rejoice and her spirit will soar when I come in the room.
> Lord Jesus Christ, I thank You for this woman. I thank You for the treasure she is, I thank You that she loves You more than me. I pray, Lord, that You will minister to her and that You will build a hedge of protection around her today. Lord Jesus Christ, we need You. All of our hope is in You.

God Is Romancing Your Wife to Himself Through You

We close with a prayer for her that is the other half of conversation with God—namely, listening for His response. God speaks through Scripture and through the prayers of His people. We offer one prayer by Michel Quoist, excerpted from his book *Prayers*.[1] Note that God is the One talking in this prayer of an adolescent or single (again) person. If you need to trust God for a wife, or if you seek to be reunited or more united with a wife God has meant for you to cherish, then pray that God will romance her to Himself through you, much as Michel Quoist models:

> It is I who made you to love,
> To love eternally;
> And your love will pass through another self of yours—
> It is she that you seek;
> Set your mind at rest; she is on your way,
>> on the way since the beginning,
>> on the way of my love.
> You must wait for her coming.
> She is approaching.
> You are approaching.
> You will recognize each other,
> For I've made her body for you, I've made yours for her.
> I've made your heart for her, I've made hers for you,
> And you seek each other, in the night,
> In "my night," which will become Light if you trust me.
>
> Keep yourself for her, son,
> As she is keeping herself for you.
> I shall keep you for one another,
> And since you hunger for love, I've put on your way all your
>> brothers to love.
> Believe me, it's a long apprenticeship, learning to love,
> And there are not several kinds of love:
> Loving is always leaving oneself to go toward others. . . .

This closing prayer by Quoist also underscores one of the hopes we have for this men's book—that God will "put on your way all your brothers to love." May God use the brothers in your study group as part of your "long apprenticeship, learning to love." May your fellow promise keepers indeed help you appreciate that God is romancing her to Himself through you, and that you will "keep yourself for her, son, as she is keeping herself for you."

WHAT DO YOU THINK?

1. What is your reaction to our models of the what, how, and why of praying with and for our wives?

   ☐ Prayer is a distraction to action; I skipped this section.
   ☐ I fell asleep reading about it, as I often do when I try praying.
   ☐ I appreciated the models; such prayers sound like love.
   ☐ I've tried everything else to make a real connection with my wife; I may as well try prayer.
   ☐ I feel awkward at prayer; Lord, teach me to pray.
   ☐ Isn't it embarrassing to be prayed for by your husband, and have those prayers broadcast before 50,000 other men and everyone else reading this book?

2. What has been your experience thus far in praying with or for your wife?

   ☐ With her, prayer is painful, because I don't like being vulnerable.
   ☐ With her, prayer is beautiful, because I am led to appreciate the inner beauty of my beloved.
   ☐ With her, prayer is purposeful, because I don't like being vulnerable.
   ☐ With her, prayer is futile, because nothing ever changes.
   ☐ With her, prayer is intimidating, because I am not very teachable.
   ☐ With her, prayer leads us into more intimacy.

3. Suppose a voice-activated tape recorder had been placed at your bedside this past week. What would your prayers for or with your wife sound like? How often would the recorder have come on? List some of your current topics for prayer, as recorded by God's tape player:

4. How do those topics for prayer compare with the three models presented in this chapter—the Apostle Paul's, Coach McCartney's, and Michel Quoist's? Any commonalties? Differences? Which one sounds most like you?

5. Of all the concerns that Paul brings to God in prayer for the ones he loves (as in Colossians 1:9-12), which are on your "Top Ten" list of things to pray for? Which items could you adopt as topics for prayer this week?

6. Do you agree with Coach Mac when he says, "Our women need a man providing the spiritual tempo and leadership in the home"? How—in practical terms—can you square this with mutual submission?

7. What problems have you experienced praying *with* your wife, as opposed to praying *for* her? Ask the group members to share their struggles and insights in this regard.

8. Go to prayer now for the men in your group and their wives. Pray in pairs, in fours, or as a whole group—but pray. Don't spend all your time soliciting requests or organizing who takes them; simply go to prayer. Use the prayer lists that each man prepared for today (see questions 3 and 5). You may also want to refer to your "Family Mission Statements."

   Pray for the man on your left, moving around the circle. Or, if you feel comfortable doing so, place those who want special prayer in the center of the whole group, or group of four, and those in the circle can lay hands on him. Pray conversationally, even concurrently, for his needs; then switch to someone else. Another way to focus your prayers is to place those "Family Mission Statements" in the center of your group and pray for them accordingly.

   Take as much time as you want for this extended prayer.

9. If time permits at the end of your session, regather and refocus your group(s) around those men who have wanted to spend more one-on-one and prayer time with their wives, but have had difficulty making this happen. Ask those men having some relative success in this area to share what they are learning from this study guide about building a successful

marriage. Remember, this is no time for preaching, but a time for apprenticing yourselves to one another.

Remember, "Since you hunger for love, I've put on your way all your brothers to love." Believe all of us who are saying, "It's a long apprenticeship, learning to love."

TRY IT AT HOME

10. Two stories in the epilogue make that final point very clear. Read it at home. Make plans beyond your present meeting together to check in with one another and extend this apprenticeship called "learning to love." Grab those calendars one last time and schedule one-on-ones—with another promise keeper and with your mate.

   This study must come to an end. This session you again prayed for one another's marriages, as you did last week. That commitment to grace need not end here. So also with your apprenticeship to love. Keep your "Family Mission Statements" handy and updated. Keep your sails unfurled, and may the wind of the Spirit always fill those sails, as you continue on the adventure of a lifetime—learning to love.

NOTE
1. Michel Quoist, *Prayers* (Kansas City, MO: Sheed and Ward, 1963, 1991), page 53.

EPILOGUE
"It's About Time"

Married life offers no panacea—if it is going to reach its potential, it will require an all-out investment by both husband and wife.
  —JAMES C. DOBSON

A successful marriage is an edifice that must be rebuilt every day.
  —ANDRÉ MAUROIS

Don't look for overnight miracles or quick fixes for your marriage. No study guide, self-help book, men's small group, or training event—no matter how creative—can provide that. Forgiveness is granted, but trust is earned. Take time for trust to rebuild and be committed to finish the race set before you. Then you will see positive changes occur in your marriage.

Something to Bank On, Something to Grow Into
None of us is perfect—just forgiven. The wives I have counseled and interviewed over the years are not expecting perfection—just consistency of effort. Wives are more than willing to forgive our failures. Though that doesn't change our past, forgiveness does change the future. Our desire as husbands who hope for the future is to live one day at a time, consistent with the way God has made us.

A lifetime of harmful patterns cannot be changed, only forgiven. However, consistent efforts from today onward will gradually heal wounds and establish new habits of success. Only loving, nurturing deposits into her emotional bank account over an extended period of time will create an atmosphere of trust that your wife can bank on.

111

Consider how a garden grows. When I was a child, I'd plant something one day and dig it up the next, just to see if it had grown any. Eventually the seedlings died, because they couldn't withstand the intensity of my efforts. What those seedlings needed was light, nutrients, some tender loving care, and enough time. I had to pull out the weeds that choked out the eventual fruit.

My marriage needs the same patience and perseverance to bear the fruit I want. By providing the necessary light, love, nutrients, and refreshing water, my wife will respond and grow closer to me. While I plant positive, growth-producing seed thoughts, I am pulling out the weeds that can choke off the fruit of our marriage—weeds of selfishness, pride, and hardness of heart.

The Case of the Ill-Timed Greeting

The longer you've neglected your marriage, and the more pain you've brought to your wife, the longer it will take your wife to trust you again. Only time will allow her to believe that the changes she sees in your life are real and will truly last.

The truth of this general principle is borne out by the story of a man who returned home from a men's conference where he was challenged to honor and love his wife. I'll call him "Ben." On the way home he decided to implement the five sure-fire principles of romancing your wife, which he had just heard about. He stopped and purchased flowers, candy, and a card. In a feat rare for many men, Ben actually read several cards to find the right one. He even knew which candy was her favorite and that she wasn't on a diet that week. Having decided to surprise his wife with all these gifts and with a sincere profession of love, Ben parked a block away from home, so he could approach in silence and preserve the element of surprise.

When he crept silently to the door and rang the bell, she answered. Wearing his best smile, Ben handed his wife the flowers, the candy, the card, and a most sincere "Honey—I love you" message. She sure was surprised but, much to his dismay, nothing else went according to plan. Instead of the warm embrace he expected, she turned away in a crumple of tears. Alarmed by this unexpected turn of events, Ben couldn't understand such a sad, almost angry, response to such overwhelming goodness on his part. After all, this well-orchestrated greeting of his, perfected with all the right gifts and smiles, was virtually guaranteed by a famous radio personality to gain the desired results.

As Ben stammered and debated with himself what to do next (they didn't prepare him for this response at the men's seminar), she choked back her tears and blurted out, "Honey, you just don't understand. When I took the kids to school in the beat-up car you left behind, it died. I had it towed and bummed a ride home. Once home, I tried to vacuum the house. Just as I was finishing up, our muddy dog tramped through, leaving quite a mess. After giving up on the car and the vacuuming, I tried the laundry—but the washing machine overflowed. To top off a depressing day, I tried cooking a nice dinner to surprise you, but I got distracted on the phone. I left dinner in the oven too long, and it burned. The smoke triggered both the smoke alarm and the sprinkler system. This hasn't been a very good day. But to make matters worse, you come home drunk!"

Poor Ben. Whether that story is true or not, it illustrates our bottom line: Your wife will need time to trust you and see that the changes are for real. Bear in mind that feelings follow action, which follows faith. If you continue to respect your wife, to honor her, to romance her, to encourage her, to have fun with her—and if you give up on quick-fix, go-for-broke romanticism—then positive changes will take place. Remember, *forgiveness is granted, but trust is earned.*

Trust implies a willingness on our part to let someone become near and dear to us. Your wife wants to give her heart and life to you. But building enough trust to make sure you will not trample it under foot—that takes time. Allow her the time she needs. She may forgive you almost immediately. But trust is earned in daily increments.

The Case of the Penitent Promise Keeper

Consider the story of a penitent promise keeper (and sometime marriage breaker) whom I met while writing this book. He came home from the National Men's Conference held at Boulder, Colorado, full of enthusiasm and determination to change things around with his wife—only to be rebuffed at the door. (This one is a true story; I'll call him "Jack.") Jack's wife remained unconvinced that Promise Keepers '93 had produced significant overnight changes in his abusive behavior, addiction problems, or broken promises. His track record of mishaps and misdeeds gave her reason to be cautious.

Despite his protests, prayers, and promises that "this time would be different," Jack found himself put to an extreme test. He had told his wife that she could count on him and that his anger was now under new management. Though she freely forgave him, he had done nothing to *earn* her trust—at least not yet. She would wait and see; in the meantime, he had to pack his bags and exit the family homestead.

Rather than let her confrontive, suspicious posture deter him from his good intentions, it stirred him up to be and do all the things that the marriage counselors and fellow promise keepers had said was so necessary. Jack cleaned up his act, bided his time, and remained faithful in prayer. He also made himself available to do the very things—and only those things—that his estranged wife could bring herself to trust him for.

He fulfilled every aspect of their visitation agreement with the kids, but kept his distance from her. When the kids needed an emergency trip to the doctor's, and she called him for help, Jack dropped everything and hustled over. When she needed to leave town and asked him to cover the bases, he was there, true to his word. When she said no to his overtures on the phone, he accepted that, keeping his anger and drinking under control.

But when she began to actually see him doing unsolicited favors and small kindnesses—running errands, treating the kids right—that left the door open to dialogue. Six months later, she invited this penitent promise keeper back into her life. Jack had earned her trust. God used that six-month probationary period to change his life of abuse and broken promises into a life of integrity and a man of action. He was not perfect and never would be, but what she saw over six months' time was the consistency of his effort, not his failures.

That was enough for her to bank on. Don't let your marriage go bankrupt for lack of deposits in your wife's emotional bank account. But if you build up an interest-bearing account with daily deposits of fun times, positive exchanges, and affirmative action, you will be rewarded with treasure in heaven that you can actually enjoy on earth. You can take that promise to the bank. Tell her Glenn and Dietrich, plus a host of other promise keepers, sent you. You won't return empty-hearted.

SEVEN PROMISES
OF A PROMISE KEEPER

Promise Keepers is a Christ-centered ministry dedicated to uniting men through vital relationships to become godly influences in their world. Throughout the nation, men are making the following commitments to become promise keepers to God in all areas of their lives. They are men who:

1. Honor Jesus Christ through prayer, worship, and obedience to His Word in the power of the Holy Spirit.
2. Pursue vital relationships with a small group of men, understanding that they need their brothers to help them keep their promises.
3. Practice spiritual, moral, ethical, and sexual purity.
4. Build strong marriages and families through love, protection, and biblical values.
5. Support the mission of their church by honoring and praying for their pastors and by actively giving their time and resources.
6. Reach beyond their own heritage to display the power of biblical unity.
7. Influence their world, being obedient to the Great Commandment (love) and the Great Commission (evangelism).

SMALL-GROUP MATERIALS FROM NAVPRESS

BIBLE STUDY SERIES

DESIGN FOR DISCIPLESHIP
GOD IN YOU
GOD'S DESIGN FOR THE FAMILY
INSTITUTE OF BIBLICAL
   COUNSELING SERIES

LEARNING TO LOVE SERIES
LIFECHANGE
LOVE ONE ANOTHER
STUDIES IN CHRISTIAN LIVING
THINKING THROUGH DISCIPLESHIP

TOPICAL BIBLE STUDIES

Becoming a Woman of
   Excellence
Becoming a Woman of Freedom
Becoming a Woman of Purpose
The Blessing Study Guide
Celebrating Life
Growing in Christ
Growing Strong in God's Family
Homemaking
Intimacy with God

Loving Your Husband
Loving Your Wife
A Mother's Legacy
Strategies for a Successful
   Marriage
Surviving Life in the Fast Lane
To Run and Not Grow Tired
To Walk and Not Grow Weary
What God Does When Men Pray
When the Squeeze Is On

BIBLE STUDIES WITH COMPANION BOOKS

Bold Love
The Feminine Journey
From Bondage to Bonding
Hiding from Love
Inside Out
The Masculine Journey
The Practice of Godliness
The Pursuit of Holiness

Secret Longings of the
   Heart
Spiritual Disciplines
Tame Your Fears
Transforming Grace
Trusting God
What Makes a Man?
The Wounded Heart
Your Work Matters to God

RESOURCES

Brothers!
How to Lead Small Groups
Jesus Cares for Women
The Small Group Leaders
   Training Course

Topical Memory System (KJV/NIV
   and NASB/NKJV)
Topical Memory System: Life
   Issues (KJV/NIV and
   NASB/NKJV)

VIDEO PACKAGES

Bold Love
Hope Has Its Reasons
Inside Out
Living Proof

Parenting Adolescents
Unlocking Your Sixth Suitcase
Your Home, A Lighthouse